W9-CGP-768

Complete Body Development with Dumbbells

Dedication

To my Father, Jonathan Z. McKown, the single most influential person in my life, my personal hero, and as Zack and Kallie say, "The best Dad in the universe".

Mark McKown

Complete Body Development with Dumbbells

Meyer & Meyer Sport

British Library Cataloguing in Publication Data
A catalogue for this book is available from the British Library

Mark McKown:
Complete Body Development with Dumbbells /
Mark McKown
– Oxford: Meyer und Meyer, (UK) Ltd., 2003
ISBN 1-84126-087-8

© 2003 by Meyer & Meyer Sport (UK) Ltd.
Aachen, Adelaide, Auckland, Budapest, Graz, Johannesburg,
Miami, Olten (CH), Oxford, Singapore, Toronto
Member of the World
Sports Publishers' Association
www.w-s-p-a.org

Printed and bound by Finidr – s. r. o. Vimperk
ISBN 1-84126-087-8
E-Mail: verlag@m-m-sports.com
www.m-m-sports.com

Table of Contents

Acknowledgements

There are many people I would like to thank for their help with the development of this book. First, I would like to thank Thomas Stengel and André Besgens as well as the rest of the staff at Meyer & Meyer Publications. I would also like to thank my good friend Greg Brittenham, Player Development Coach for the New York Knicks (and the best in the business) for his invaluable input, suggestions and help.

No book of this type is complete without the input and feedback of other experts in the field. With this in mind, I relied on the knowledge and expertise of the following friends and colleagues; Bill Barfield, Ph.D., Medical University of South Carolina; Jeff Watkinson, MS, CSCS, Head Strength Coach for Basketball, University of Missouri; John Godwin, MS, CSCS, Head Strength and Conditioning Coach, College of Charleston (SC); and Rich King MS, CSCS, of the Carolina Athletic Development Center.

I would also like to thank Larry Miller, Owner, Dennis Haslam, President, and Kevin O'Connor, General Manager of the Utah Jazz for allowing me to be a part of the best organization in pro sports, and for the opportunity to work on this project. Ed Rosenberger, a true genius with the camera, took the cover photo, as well as all photos in this book. I am grateful for Ed's help and magic with the camera. I would also like to thank the models Adam, Rachael, Zack and Kallie for their patience, endurance and ability to help the photo shoot flow smoothly.

I would be amiss if I did not recognize the help, support and guidance I have received from Jerry Sloan, Head Coach of the Utah Jazz, and perennial NBA All Star, Karl Malone. These two men define the word *friend* for me, and represent what is "right" about professional sports.

Last, but definitely not least, I would like to thank my wife, Sonja, and my children, Zack and Kallie, for providing me with support, understanding, valuable feedback, and the motivation to write this book.

Foreword

In 1997 the Utah Jazz hired the organization's first fulltime coach in charge of the strength training, conditioning and athletic development of our team. Mark McKown came to us with a rich background in these areas, as well as experience as a college basketball player and coach. I thought then, and know now, the Jazz found the perfect match for our team and organization.

In a short period of time Mark has proved to be a very valuable asset. Perhaps his best attribute is his ability to successfully work with and motivate the professional athlete. As any experienced NBA coach will tell you, this is not always an easy task. This trait, along with his innovative techniques in the weight room, on the court, and other training venues make him a unique coach, and among the very best in his profession.

When I was a player in the league you were left to your own resources when it came to the physical preparation to play. I was always willing to work at getting better as a player, and I learned early in my career that proper conditioning and training could mean the difference in a fair season and a "successful" season for me personally. I wish I knew then what I know now, and I wish I had a coach like Mark to guide me. I am positive that my career would have lasted longer, and I would have experienced fewer injuries if I had benefited from the type of training he does with our players today.

Complete Body Development with Dumbbells represents Mark's style. It is innovative, easy to read and follow, and very informative. This book will provide you with a route to making the kind of personal gains you are seeking, while utilizing many of the same exercises used by our Jazz players.

Jerry Sloan
Head Coach
Utah Jazz
February 2002

Preface

When speaking to groups of coaches, athletes, fans, or talking with representatives of the media, most of the questions I receive are in reference to Karl Malone. The reasons for these questions are obvious. Karl is one of the best athletes to ever play the game of basketball, he is a perennial all star, one of the strongest athletes in professional sports, and he has, without a doubt, the best physique in the NBA. In addition to all these attributes, his ability to control his 6'9" 265 lb. body is legendary. Karl gives credit for much of his physical success to his solid work in the weight room, which consists of 70% dumbbell training.

I cannot guarantee that you will develop a body, strength or control like a Karl Malone by training predominately with dumbbells. However, no matter what your body is like now you can make significant gains via work with dumbbells. The degree to which you improve will be dependent upon your efforts, the training program you follow and your genetic potential. This book will introduce you to the means to developing a great individualized program and the keys to focusing your efforts. Your parents, however, have predetermined your genetic potential.

Keep in mind that no matter what your genetic potential, you can make improvements, and that dumbbell training is one of the most efficient approaches to maximizing your physical potential. It may help by viewing your potential as your own personal mountain. Your ultimate goal is to get as close to the peak as possible. In the athletic world we see folks out – perform their opponents or teammates regularly, even though their potential (or personal mountain) may not be as great.

It is the intent of this book to help you reach your peak via the fastest, safest, and most efficient route – dumbbell training. The benefits of, and best approaches to, dumbbell training will be addressed in detail. In short, however, I can tell you that training with dumbbells is an excellent route to good muscle balance and symmetry, thus a better physique, increased muscle size and strength, and improved overall body control.

CHAPTER 1

Common Questions (And Not so Common Answers)

There is an abundance of misinformation surrounding exercise and fitness. This is due in part to the fact that strength training, exercise, and fitness are not absolute sciences. In other words, contradictions exist in the literature with respect to the specifics of development of optimal health and fitness. However, there are established standards that we now understand to be sound and reliable when it comes to developing the body. This is because research related to the health and physical development of humans has advanced light years in just the past decade.

Establishing an accurate knowledge base is essential before undertaking any new investment. Would you purchase a car without knowing how to drive it? Most likely the answer is no. Yet, the vast majority of people (including a surprising number of professional athletes) purchase health club memberships or expensive equipment without the adequate know how to properly use them. Folks want to re-sculpt their bodies, enhance their strength, or improve their overall health, but they really don't know the most effective means of accomplishing their goals. This question and answer section will help you become better informed, thus better prepared to invest in developing your body via dumbbell training.

What are the advantages of training with dumbbells?

Dumbbell training offers what is perhaps the best all-around approach to body building/sculpting, strength training, athletic development, and improved body control and coordination. This is due in part to the fact that dumbbells allow you to train the various sides of the body equally. For example, dumbbell curls will offer equal resistance to both arms, thus taxing the biceps equally. Conversely, performing curls with a barbell, or curl bar will allow the dominant arm to perform a predominate amount of the work when executing the lift.

Dumbbells also offer one of the best avenues to functional training. In other words, the instability created by dumbbell training forces the body to constantly seek balance. This in turn helps you develop body control and balance. Dumbbells also allow you to develop strength through multiple planes of motion. The result is improved balance, body control, and multiple range strength. Thus, you are capable of functioning better in your day to day environment.

Dumbbells require relatively little space; thus they are very convenient for the "at home" lifter. Last, but not least, they provide a safe avenue for resistance training.

What type of dumbbells are available for my use?

There are a wide variety of dumbbells on the market. For home use many people choose to use vinyl-covered dumbbells. These dumbbells usually come in bright colors and designed to protect floors from dents and carpet tears. Vinyl covered dumbbells usually do not come in weights much higher than 20 lbs. There are also adjustable dumbbells in which the weight can be adjusted by adding or taking off weight plates. These dumbbells do not take up much space, but are a bit inconvenient due to the necessity of attaching and removing weights and then securing them with some type of end clamp.

One of the more space efficient and versatile types of dumbbells is marketed under the name Power Blocks. These dumbbells work by inserting a pin in the weight you have selected to use. This takes just a few seconds. You can adjust the weight of each dumbbell in various increments. There are models that adjust from 3 to 21 pounds (3-pound increments), 2.5 to 45 pounds (2.5-pound increments), or 5 to 45 pounds (5-pound increment.

In most health clubs, athletic training centers, and commercial facilities you will usually find solid dumbbells made of cast iron or steel. Also somewhat common in these types of facilities is steel or iron dumbbells encased in rubber. The cast iron dumbbells routinely come with a hexagonal shaped head. The steel dumbbells come with weight plates attached by a bolt or welded to a solid handle, or occasionally in one solid (molded) piece.

The handles of these dumbbells are most often solid, round and offer 6 inches of space for grasping. There are some handles that are fatter in the middle and offer the lifter a more accommodating grip. There is also a new design handle that is somewhat triangular in shape with rounded corners. These handles are less likely to rotate or slip in the hand during use. Most handles have rough, or knurled, surfaces to also help reduce the risk of the dumbbells slipping or rotating in the lifter's hand.

What accessories, or other equipment, will I need in order to properly train with dumbbells?

An adjustable bench is practically a requirement for the dumbbell trainer. Most benches of this type offer a back that adjusts from zero to eighty-five degrees, and a seat also designed to change angles to accommodate the lifter's needs. Numerous exercises can only be performed on a dumbbell bench or similar item of equipment.

You may wish to invest in lifting gloves to reduce the development of hand calluses, and to aid in grasping the dumbbell. Most gloves are made of leather or a durable heavy fabric blend and have reinforced palms and open fingers.

Weight belts are another option you may consider, but they are probably not necessary unless you have a lower back ailment, or your physician has prescribed one for use. Weight belts are typically constructed of leather with a metal buckle, or heavy synthetic webbing with a metal buckle and Velcro fastener.

As you advance in your training you may wish to invest in a wobble board and/or a stability ball. These two apparatus are ideal for performing a wide variety of exercises that require the incorporation of balance and body control. This in turn is an ideal approach for enhancing your ability to function better – whether it is carrying the groceries into the house, or sprinting down the basketball court. Exercises specifically designed for these two pieces of equipment will be discussed in detail in chapters 11 and 12.

What is the single best routine for improved health and appearance?

There is no "one size fits all" exercise routine. It is important to note that individuals respond differently to various exercise routines. What may be a great program for you may only be fair for your friend or training partner. As you advance in your training you will see that your body seems to respond better to certain exercise programs. One thing that is certain is that your body seems to respond best when exposed to variety of training routines. Your body basically grows bored or stagnates if it is hit with the same exercise stimulus day after day. *So when it comes to exercise, variety truly is the spice of life.* As you progress through this book you will find that variety and simplicity are usually the best approach. In other words, you can get a better body without becoming bored, or getting lost in the confusing maze of fitness jargon.

If I work as hard as an athlete like Karl Malone or Gabriel Reese, in a program comparable his or hers, will I develop a physique like his/hers?

That is a tough question, because it depends on your own personal genetic code. As was mentioned earlier in this book, not everyone has the potential for a championship physique, yet everyone has the potential to improve. The bottom line is this – train smart and consistently and you will make very noticeable physical (not to mention emotional/mental) gains.

What factors determine my potential for a better physique?

We all know people who have nice physiques that do little if anything to develop their bodies (which does not necessarily mean that they are "healthy"). These folks represent the segment of our population that has tremendous physical potential. Most of us, however fall into the group that must "work" to develop our bodies.

1. *Muscle fiber type.* There are three types of skeletal muscles in the human body, slow twitch (type I), and fast twitch (type IIa, type IIb). Muscles (i.e., biceps, triceps, quadriceps, etc.) are composed of combinations of these fibers. Most people have a fairly equal distribution of fast and slow twitch muscle fiber. Many experts believe people with a higher percentage of fast twitch muscle fiber are more likely to experience muscle size gains (hypertrophy) than those with a high percentage of slow twitch muscle fiber. Folks with more slow twitch muscle fiber will have greater potential for endurance type activities, like distance running. Since slow twitch and fast twitch muscle fibers are randomly arranged in the muscles it is next to impossible to accurately determine ones' percentage of fiber distribution. Of course if you are willing to invest in, and then go through, extensive muscle biopsies, a reasonably accurate assessment of muscle fiber type can be determined. We do not recommend this.

2. *Frame size/body type.* Generally successful body builders, power lifters, and Olympic lifters have big frames. People with wide shoulders, a big rib cage, and large wrists inherit a frame that is usually well-suited for strength training and body building. Yet whether you are tall or short, wide or slender you still have the potential to improve your physique.

3. *Sex.* There is one major reason why men are typically stronger and have bigger muscles than women. Testosterone plays a major role in strength and muscle hypertrophy (size gains). We should point out, however, that some research has suggested that women have equal relative potential for leg strength to that of males. Generally speaking however, men are going to have greater potential for muscle size and strength. Yet women in the last twenty years, or so have shown that they can make impressive physical gains. No longer is it considered non-feminine to be strong and muscular.

4. *Age.* The bottom line is that regardless of your age you can make physical gains in strength, muscle size and body control. Young children are not going to make large hypertrophy gains, but can make significant strength gains. This is particularly true following puberty. The geriatric population can make impressive gains in strength, as well as muscle hypertrophy. As a matter of fact, resistance training has been shown to increase the body's testosterone production in all adults. This in turn increases the rate at which we develop physically.

Muscle fiber type, frame size, sex, and age do not represent all the factors affecting your potential for a better physique. They are, however, the major determinants that you have no control over. Your training approach, how often you train, and what you eat (nutrition) are keys to your potential that you do have control over.

Remember, no matter what your genetic make up, you can improve your physical fitness and appearance – which will in turn lead to many other health benefits.

Will the muscle I build turn to fat if I stop dumbbell training?

No. Muscle and fat are two totally different types of tissue. If you stop training you will probably accumulate more body fat and the muscle tissue you have built will atrophy (this is the opposite of hyperthrophy, meaning that a cross sectional area of your muscles will get smaller).

Your body (muscles particularly) adapts to resistance training. Muscles adapt by increasing in size (hypertrophy) and by becoming more efficient. If you cease resistance training, or even cut back, the muscle becomes smaller (atrophy), because the demand is less. A reduction (or stoppage) in resistance training usually means you burn less calories thus you will probably accumulate more fat. It is also important to know that as your muscle mass (size) increases so does your resting metabolic rate. In other words, bigger/stronger muscles mean you burn more calories – at rest and work.

What is resistance training?

Anytime you move a load with the intent of obtaining some sort of physical benefit you are participating in resistance training. Weight training is one type of resistance training, and includes any type of exercise in which you apply force to move a specific external object. When you lift dumbbells, barbells, or work with weight machines you are weight training. Weight lifting is a term usually (but not absolutely) used to describe Olympic-type lifting. The Olympic lifts are the clean and jerk, and the snatch. Variations of these lifts include: hang cleans, power cleans, and push presses. Power lifting is another type of weight training and includes the bench press, dead lift, and squat. Strength training is designed specifically with the intent of increasing your ability to move a load, and overlaps with power lifting and Olympic lifting. Bodybuilding is generally accomplished via weight training and includes an approached designed to increase muscle size and reduce body fat. Resistance training also includes body weight exercises like push-ups, pull-ups, lunge walks, and even crunches.

What is functional training?

The roots of functional training started within the rehabilitation and physical therapy settings. The concept being to get the patient back to his/her activity via exercises designed to complement the persons' most common movements and activities.

It stands to reason that functional training for a healthy individual will produce enhanced ability to move and function in their normal environment. For example, The busy parent will be able to better interact with their children in active situations. The retired schoolteacher will be able to shop, get in out of the car, and work in the yard with greater ease. The athlete will respond to functional training with an enhanced ability to sprint, jump, change directions and control his/her body.

Will resistance training make a female develop a masculine appearance?

No. Actually resistance training can assist women/girls in becoming more feminine by enhancing their body composition, improving their posture, not to mention boosting their self image.

Unfortunately, some (a very small percentage) female body builders, and athletes have a masculine appearance. As we mentioned earlier, the male hormone testosterone determines the degree of someone's masculinity. If a female abuses anabolic steroids, their testosterone levels increase and they develop masculine characteristics.

Wouldn't my mother be better off doing aerobics than dumbbell training?

Not necessarily – In addition to an improved physical appearance as a result of less body fat and increases in lean muscle your mother will experience numerous health benefits via resistance training. Resistance training will increase her muscle mass, which will increase her resting metabolic rate. Thus she will burn more calories during the course of a day. She will also experience a greater ease of movement due to the strength gains she will realize.

Tasks like walking the dog, climbing stairs, or carrying groceries will become easier. Some research reflects that she may very well receive cardiovascular benefits as a result of her training, too. Perhaps the greatest benefit she will receive from resistance exercise will be an increase in bone density. Not only will the negative consequences of osteoporosis be attenuated; these negative effects can actually be reversed. This does not occur with aerobic training alone.

Should females resistance train differently than males?

No. Although there are some physiological differences between the sexes (i.e. pelvic width and shoulder width) there is no reason why women cannot train as intensely using the same exercises as men. As we mentioned earlier, women are not going to experience hypertrophy at the same rate as men, but other physical gains (i.e. strength) will be relatively the same.

Will dumbbell training allow me to target where I lose fat?

No. The only true way to spot reduce is by lipo suction – which we do not recommend. In other words, if you feel your buttocks are too fat and you train religiously on a machine designed to target your glutes, you will increase your glute strength and burn extra calories. However, your body will not specifically use the fat in your bottom as fuel for this activity.

What is the best way to lose body fat?

Quite simply, burn more calories than you take in. The best way to accomplish this is through a sound exercise routine (one that will elevate your heart rate for 20 plus minutes) and a healthy diet.

Will dumbbell training make me "muscle bound"?

No. This is another myth perpetuated by uninformed people. Actually resistance training can help improve your flexibility, if you train through a full range of motion. For example, when a healthy person performs a dumbbell bench press they can help their flexibility by allowing the dumbbell to go deep enough to stretch the pectoralis and anterior deltoid muscles (the muscles in the chest and shoulder). Competitive weight lifters are perhaps the best example of the flexibility benefits you can receive from resistance training. They are routinely one of the most flexible group of athletes at Olympic competitions.

Will dumbbell training help my cardiovascular fitness?

This will surprise some people — but the answer is yes. Research has demonstrated that serious resistance trainers experience a healthy increase in the thickness of the heart's left ventricular wall. This helps the heart pump blood more efficiently. Also, certain types of dumbbell training (i.e. super set training) can be designed to enhance your aerobic capacity, which will obviously help your cardiovascular fitness.

Will dumbbell training make me run and react slower?

If resistance training is your only activity then the answer is probably yes, because you will be training your body at a slow speed. However, if you combine dumbbell training with other activities like running or cycling then you may very well improve your speed of movement.

Will dumbbell training hurt my coordination?

No - just the opposite will happen. As a result of resistance training your body control will be enhanced - particularly if you train with dumbbells. Your ability to recover from a trip or stumble, or to change direction on the field or court will improve as your strength improves. Even simple tasks like getting in and out of the car and climbing the stairs become easier.

Is there one dumbbell exercise I can do that will strengthen my entire body?

No. There are exercises that require the use of multiple muscle groups, but there is not one exercise that offers the total strength-training package. As we will discuss later on, one of the keys to a successful strengthening/body-sculpting program is training for muscle balance. This means that you should train your upper body relative to your lower body, biceps equal to your triceps, your quads equal to your hamstrings, etc.

Is it possible to "sculpt" (or "tone") my body without increasing the size of my muscles?

Yes. This requires a program designed to help you burn body fat and increase strength while experiencing very limited muscle hypertrophy. There are various approaches you can use to reach this goal. Circuit training using relatively light to moderate resistance (weight) for high repetitions (15-20), with short rest periods between sets (30-45 seconds) is one approach that is conducive to toning with most people. You may find however, that this approach is not best suited for you. If that is the case you can use this book to help you design a different personal program.

Is dumbbell training, by itself, enough for total fitness?

No. Although you can make significant fitness gains via dumbbell training, it does not provide for all your fitness needs. For example, a thirty-year-old businessperson would be well advised to include flexibility work, as well as aerobic conditioning into their regular exercise routine. Even though they may be receiving some of these benefits via their resistance training, it is not enough to make significant gains in these other very important fitness components. Competitive athletes should focus on sport specific conditioning (i.e. anaerobic fitness: speed, explosive movement, and body control development, etc.).

Is it better to dumbbell train or to do aerobic activity to reduce my body fat?

In an ideal world you would do both, as this is the best approach (along with a healthy diet) to losing fat. Many exercise scientists feel that for your body to burn fat during exercise you must train aerobically. There is no question that the research supports the use of low intensity, long duration activity for fat reduction. However, there is research that also supports the use of interval type training (i.e. dumbbell circuit training) as the best approach to fat reduction (some experts say interval training is even better than aerobic activity). The idea is that this will elevate your heart rate significantly and burn more calories than an aerobic type activity.

Is it better to resistance train on machines or with dumbbells?

There is definitely a common opinion among most strength and conditioning specialists toward the use of free weights, or dumbbells. This opinion is well founded, as the use of dumbbells forces you to control and balance your movements, where as weight machines generally do not. When you have to control your movements you develop the synergistic muscles (the muscles that must support and assist in a movement). The use of dumbbells can allow for more functional type training. In other words, you can better prepare for your normal daily activities (i.e. walking, running, climbing, lifting, and combinations of activities).

However, the use of weight machines is also very worthwhile. They provide a great opportunity for beginners to get acclimated to lifting, because they are safer and easy to control. Machines allow for better isolation of specific muscle groups, which is often ideal for the person interested in sculpting their body. Weight machines also offer resistance without the need for a spotter, which can benefit many people.

Is it necessary to dumbbell train everyday to make gains?

No. As a matter of fact it is possible to make strength gains and physique improvements training as little as twice a week. How often you train depends upon your experience and how your body responds to exercise, particularly resistance training. Competitive body builders will workout up to 6 days a week utilizing a variety of routines. Quite often they will train two body parts per session. For example, session one may be devoted to the legs and trunk, session two the chest and back, and session three shoulders and arms. By focusing on only two body parts per session they allow the muscles time to recover between workouts. Of course not all body builders use this approach. Some will train the total body 3 days a week; others will train 4 days a week attacking the upper body during one session and the lower body during the next. Yet others will workout for 3 straight days and take a day or two off between lifting sessions. Power and Olympic lifters usually (but not always) resistance train 3 to 4 days a week. They, too, have a variety of approaches to their training.

Design a plan of attack that will allow you to meet your goals, while fitting in your schedule. Chapter 5 will help you do just that, as it focuses on choosing and organizing your routine.

I train regularly with my partner, following the same routine and training at the same level of intensity. Why aren't my gains in strength and muscle size as great as his?

Quite frankly your friend may have a genetic make up that is going to allow him to make better gains in these physical categories than you. However, this does not mean that you are incapable of making significant gains as well. You should also take into consideration that the "one size fits all" approach to strength training is not for everyone. Your body may respond better to another approach. Change routines periodically until you find one that you feel best meets your individual needs.

I seem to get a great deal of muscle soreness after my dumbbell training sessions, is this normal?

When first starting a resistance training program muscle soreness is quite common. Muscle soreness will also be associated with new exercises to experienced lifters. The soreness is a result of micro tears within the muscle itself. The soreness is not a result of a lactic acid build up in the muscles, as many folks believe.

Pay attention to this soreness - if it persists over a long period of time visit your doctor. For immediate relief drink large quantities of water (minimum of eight glasses a day) and ice the sore area for 10 to 20 minutes after workouts. Prior to working out, warm-up using movement patterns that mimic the exercise you are about to undertake. For example, if you are going to do dumbbell presses, warm-up with a light set of push-ups. Follow this with some stretching of the muscles that are sore (i.e. pectoralis muscles).

Will dumbbell training hurt my young child?

Not if done correctly. Resistance training potentially could be very beneficial for your youngster. Contrary to what many people would have you believe, children are not at a high risk for injury when they resistance train in a safe, supervised and structured environment.

Children from six to thirteen should train with sub-maximal resistance (light weights), for sub-maximal, yet fairly high (ten +) repetitions. Also it should be made a positive experience, allowing the children the freedom to experience this activity of their own volition.

Will I ever get to the point where I can stop exercising?

Exercise should be a regular part of your life. The health benefits associated with regular workouts are well documented.

Unfortunately you can not stock pile your training sessions. In other words, your body needs the stimulus of exercise in order to improve. If you stop exercising you will lose what you have gained significantly faster than the time it took to develop it. Actually in as little as six to eight weeks of inactivity your body and health can regress to where it was prior to you beginning your resistance-training program. As we mentioned in this chapter consistency is a major key to success.

Is it possible to train at the same level of difficulty and maintain what I have?

Probably not. Your body is constantly adapting to its environment. Exposed to a new stimulus the body will seek to reach a homeostatic state. Expose the body to the same routine over and over again and it no longer finds it necessary to adapt. This is because it has found the most physically economical means of dealing with this part of its environment. In other words, your muscles grow bored and are no longer stimulated to grow. They have become more efficient and can perform the same work utilizing less energy. If you find yourself gaining a few extra pounds of body fat yet you haven't changed your eating habits or exercise routine, a static training stimulus may be the cause.

The answer to this dilemma is to follow a progression that is included in our dumbbell training guidelines in chapter 4. The principle of progressive overload - means placing a systematic increase in the demands you place upon the body. When it gets fairly easy to complete a set on the bench, for example, then you should progress by either increasing the weight or the number of repetitions you perform.

Will running or cycling offer the same benefits to my legs as resistance training?

No, but you may be surprised to know that you can make impressive hypertrophic gains via certain exercises like cycling, skating, running (sprinting), and stair climbing. Folks who engage in the previous mentioned activities on a regular basis have awesomely developed legs – whether they resistance train with weights or not. However these activities by themselves will not "totally" develop your legs. In order to increase strength it is necessary to train with a greater resistance than these activities offer. Also to develop muscle balance weight training is necessary. We would also point out that to experience optimal muscle size gains, resistance training with free weights and/or weight machines is most certainly necessary.

What does the term muscle balance mean?

The term muscle balance refers to training and developing the various muscles and regions of the body with a relative equal approach. For example, you should train your lower body equal to your upper body, your back equal to your chest, and your biceps equal to your triceps and so on.

How long before I start seeing results from my dumbbell training?

Initially (in the first week) you may actually feel a little weaker as your body adjusts and compensates due to the "new" stimulus. Starting as soon as two weeks (usually around four to six weeks though) you will start experiencing strength gains. These will be neuromuscular gains - meaning your body adapts by utilizing more of the muscle you have in order to move a load. In other words, your nervous system will communicate more efficiently with your muscles resulting in an increased capacity to do work. Around six to eight weeks you will start seeing the fruits of your labors in the form of enhanced muscle "tone" and muscle hypertrophy (size).

CHAPTER 2
Know Your Body

Ask a NASCAR driver about his cars' engine and he will respond with specifics that you may think only a mechanic would know. This knowledge is key to his success on the track. Failure on the driver's part to recognize the slightest change in the engine's sound or performance may lead to failure. You can bet your bottom dollar that these people have no problem identifying the alternator, carburetor or radiator on their cars.

Yet most fitness enthusiast do not share a comparable knowledge of their bodies. The majority of exercise buffs do not know the difference between tendons and ligaments, or the deltoids and the rhomboids and how they work. It is critical to your fitness success to understand the body and how it works. The bottom line: it is important to become familiar with the body's' basic musculature and how those muscles function prior to beginning an exercise program.

Muscle Actions and Movements

The basic function of skeletal muscle is to provide movement for the body. There are approximately 600 muscles in the body, and the majority of them are used for body movement. Around fifty percent of your weight is from skeletal muscle.

Movement occurs as a result of muscle contractions. Quite simply, when a muscle contracts it shortens and causes movement. This type of muscle movement is called a concentric action. For example, when raising the weight while performing a dumbbell curl, a concentric muscle action is taking place in the biceps brachia (we use this example because just about all guys dig working their biceps). When you lower the dumbbell, the biceps must supply constant tension in order to control the weights descent. The muscle action that takes place while lowering a resistance is called an eccentric action. Quite often the concentric action is called the positive part of an exercise and the eccentric phase the negative.

When raising the weight during the dumbbell chest press, concentric muscle actions are taking place in the pectoralis muscles of the chest, the deltoids of the shoulders and the triceps of the arm. When lowering the resistance, the same muscles supply tension while lengthening - this is an eccentric muscle action.

You are significantly stronger eccentrically than concentrically. This is one of your body's protective mechanisms. For example when jumping down from a 3-foot platform to the ground you must absorb close to three times your body weight. For a 150-pound person this amounts to approximately 450 pounds of force. This is a somewhat easy task for most healthy individuals. Yet, the average 150-pound person would struggle (or maybe get crushed) attempting to perform a squat with 450 pounds.

A skeletal muscle is made up of hundreds of muscle fibers or muscle cells - much like a cotton rope is made up of hundreds of smaller threads. Each muscle fiber is relatively long and thin like the threads of the rope. Within the fibers are other thread-like structures called myofibrils. Each myofibril is made up of sarcomeres, which are attached end to end. The microscopic level is where the muscle contraction occurs. Within the sarcomere are myofilaments called actin and myosin. The idea behind how muscle contraction takes place is called the sliding filament theory and involves an interaction between these two myofilaments. Basically what is believed to happen is that the actin filament slides over the myosin filament when a message is received from the nervous system. When you curl a dumbbell this is what takes place in the biceps during the concentric phase. When lowering the dumbbell the eccentric action is easier because the actin and myosin are reluctant to separate.

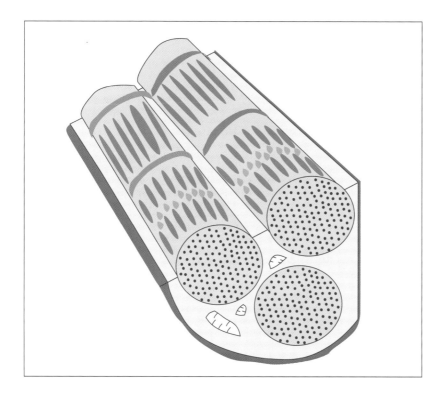

Have you ever experienced muscle pain and soreness after resistance training session? If so, you probably have had someone (maybe even an exercise expert) tell you the pain is a result of a lactic acid buildup in your muscles. Lactic acid is a byproduct produced by the muscles during fairly intense bouts of exercise.

Actually your pain is probably the result of micro tears within the muscle. These tears occur during eccentric work and stimulate muscle repair and growth. They are key to your training success.

One school of thought is that when you experience quite a bit of eccentric work micro tears occur. When the actin filament is forcefully pulled away from the myosin filament soreness results. The action of separating the actin from the myosin during the eccentric phase of a lift can be compared to a struggle with "Chinese handcuffs". When you place your index fingers in either end of the handcuffs and attempt to pull them apart the handcuffs lock in place. The harder you pull the greater the resistance. The same is true in the case of the sliding filaments. The greater the force, the stronger the actin and myosin bond. When they are pulled apart via exercise soreness is a probable result. The difficulty to separate these filaments protects you from injury when running, jumping, lifting, throwing etc.

The Musculoskeletal System

Skeletal muscles move the bones as a result of conscious thought. They do not create movement by themselves. The nervous system sends the muscles a message and they in turn contract to move a bone. Muscles are attached to bones by tendons. In turn, ligaments attach the bones to one another. There are also cardiac muscles (found only in the heart) and smooth muscle (found in the walls of blood vessels and digestive tract). These two types of muscle are considered involuntary as they act without conscious thought. The focus of this book is obviously on skeletal muscle.

Your body is capable of a wide range of movements. This is because your skeletal system is made up of levers. When the muscles act upon (pulling the bone) one of these levers movements occurs. You are capable of a wide variety of movements. The most common of these movements are flexion and extension. When a joint angle decreases, as in a dumbbell curl, it is called flexion. When the joint angle increases, as in a triceps pushdown, it is called extension.

Extension

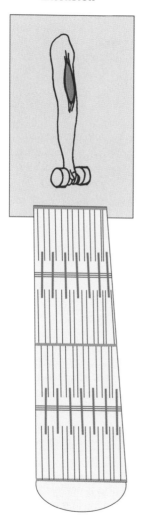

Eccentric

Flexion

Concentric

Muscle Fiber Recruitment

As was mentioned earlier, initial strength gains are neuromuscular in nature. In other words, your body adapts to the stimulus of resistance training by recruiting additional muscle fibers to assist in completing the task of moving the load. For example, it will take more of the biceps muscle fibers to curl a 20-pound dumbbell than it will to lift a glass of water to your mouth. In both of these situations, however, the fibers that are used contract completely. This is called the all or none principle. Fibers do not partially contract. The fibers receive a message from a nerve to act and they do, totally.

Each muscle has hundreds of sites where the nerves can innervate (process of stimulating) the fibers. These sites are called motor units (MU). Each MU controls a certain number of muscle fibers. As you train, these motor units become more efficient and are capable of bringing more muscle fibers into play when performing resistance exercises. This allows you to generate more force, which makes it possible for you to lift more weight.

Muscle Hypertrophy and Atrophy

When your muscles are forced to repeatedly work harder than normal they adapt by increasing in size. This is called hypertrophy. The larger a muscle fiber the greater its capacity for work.

Men tend to experience greater gains in muscle size than women do. This is primarily due to greater amounts of the male hormone testosterone in their systems. It is also believed that males generally have more muscle fibers per muscle than females.

There is a direct correlation between muscle fiber size and your ability to generate force, or demonstrate strength. So when someone points out a body builder to you and says, "he is just big, but not strong", don't believe it. Body-builders train specifically for increases in muscle size, but they also have the capability to generate a great deal of force. By the same token, power lifters and Olympic lifters may not have the muscle symmetry and definition of body builders, but they do have very large muscles – which is key to their ability to lift heavy weights.

Work your muscles and they will get bigger. Don't work them and they will get smaller. Atrophy is the term used to define "wasting away", or a decrease in a muscle fiber cross-sectional area. You do not lose the number of muscle fibers you have – it is just the ones you do have shrink. If you have ever worn a cast on an injured arm or leg then you probably witnessed first hand the results of muscle inactivity – atrophy.

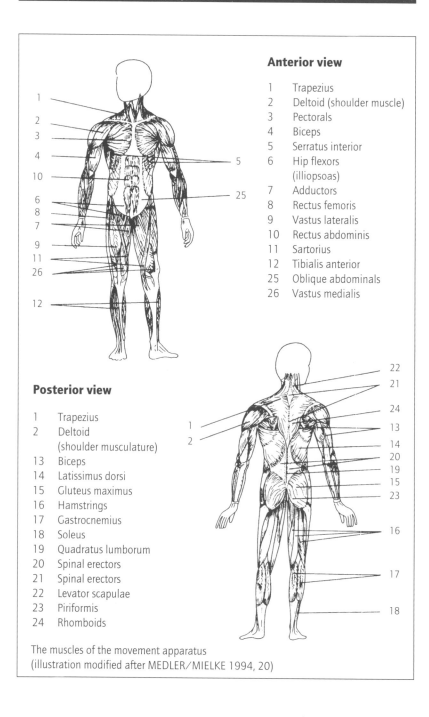

Anterior view

1   Trapezius
2   Deltoid (shoulder muscle)
3   Pectorals
4   Biceps
5   Serratus interior
6   Hip flexors
    (illiopsoas)
7   Adductors
8   Rectus femoris
9   Vastus lateralis
10 Rectus abdominis
11 Sartorius
12 Tibialis anterior
25 Oblique abdominals
26 Vastus medialis

Posterior view

1   Trapezius
2   Deltoid
    (shoulder musculature)
13 Biceps
14 Latissimus dorsi
15 Gluteus maximus
16 Hamstrings
17 Gastrocnemius
18 Soleus
19 Quadratus lumborum
20 Spinal erectors
21 Spinal erectors
22 Levator scapulae
23 Piriformis
24 Rhomboids

The muscles of the movement apparatus
(illustration modified after MEDLER/MIELKE 1994, 20)

CHAPTER 3

Building the Foundation with Dumbbell Training

Your body is much like a building in that it is dependent upon a good solid foundation for support. Without a well-built base, you will be less sturdy, subject to premature structural breakdown, unable to handle intense outside forces, restricted from growth, and much less functional. A building's foundation is built through the efforts of man and machine with materials such as concrete, steel, and brick. Your foundation is built via resistance training. This training typically takes place in the weight room, but, as you will see in chapter 11, there are other avenues to building a sturdy base. Bone, muscle and connective tissues (ligaments and tendons) support your structure.

Your foundation equates to your strength. The stronger you are, the greater your ability to exert force and to function. Yet, the benefits associated with building a strong foundation are not limited to strength alone. Other positive aspects associated with dumbbell training include gains in muscle size (hypertrophy), improved muscle tone, greater strength endurance, increased muscle power, reduced risk of injury, better body control, improved posture, increased metabolic rate, improved flexibility, better overall appearance, and a higher degree of self esteem.

Specific Benefits and Adaptations of Dumbbell Training

Increased Muscle (tendon, ligament) Strength – The first reward you see from dumbbell training is an increase in muscle strength (the ability to exert force). Your body is a very efficient machine. When repeatedly exposed to a new stimulus it will seek to adapt. If that stimulus is a heavy load increased muscle strength is the natural adaptation.

Your initial strength gains are due to neuromuscular adaptations. In other words, your muscles repeatedly receive the message, "heavy load" and respond by bringing more muscle fibers into play. Simply stated, your nervous system learns to recruit more muscle fibers in order to exert force. These changes typically occur in the first four to six weeks of training. As you progress in your resistance training program, you will receive additional strength gains as a result of increases in muscle fiber size.

Not only do your muscles get stronger, your tendons and ligaments adapt with an increased strength as well. This adaptation increases joint stability and reduces your risk of injury.

Building a solid strength base is important for body builders, athletes, and toners, as well as strength trainers. Enhancing your strength does not mean that you need to establish various lifting maximums (i.e. bench press max). However, if one of your goals is to establish personal bests in certain lifts, then we suggest that the bulk of your training involves heavy weight (70% - 90% of your 1 Rep Max) for low repetitions (2 - 8), with long rest periods (2 to 3 minutes) between sets.

NOTE: We will go into a detailed explanation of how to reach your various goals (i.e. muscle size, strength, power, etc.) in chapter 4.

Muscle Fiber Recruitment

In order to move a load specific muscles must act. For example, if you are performing a shoulder press, the deltoids, trapezius, and triceps must contract in order to lift the bar. Messages are sent to muscle fibers within the muscle triggering them to act with a concentric action. When a muscle fiber contracts it does so totally. There are no partial contractions. This is called the all or none principle.

Muscle fiber contractions generate the force that allows you to move the load. If the task is somewhat difficult then your body will recruit more muscle fibers to assist. For instance, when lifting a 20-pound dumbbell during a curl many fibers within the biceps must contract. Perform a similar movement with a glass of water and significantly less muscle fibers are recruited.

Muscle Hypertrophy – Strength gains also come as a result of muscle hypertrophy. This is an increase on muscle fiber size. As a fiber becomes larger its ability to generate force increases. Around the six-week mark you may start noticing changes in your muscle size. A program of high repetitions (8-16), and short rest periods (1.5 minutes and less) is conducive to muscle hypertrophy. There are various approaches to incorporating this guideline. We will share some of these with you in chapter 4.

Improved Muscle Tone – Muscle tone is a term used by some fitness trainers and in many health clubs across the country. In general people who wish to "tone" hope to improve their physical appearance without becoming bulky. This entails a reduction of body fat and an increase in muscle resilience. This cannot happen without some gains in muscle hypertrophy. The idea of ones muscles getting bigger seems to terrify people who wish to "tone". This is probably because they visualize their body becoming too big and bulky. If you follow the appropriate guidelines this will not happen.

A program consisting of relatively high reps (12-20) and short rest periods between sets is best for "toning". This approach in conjunction with a healthy diet results in a reduction of body fat and a subtle change in muscle hypertrophy - or better muscle tone.

Greater Muscle Strength Endurance – Strength endurance refers to the ability to generate force over a long period of time. Competitive rowers are an excellent example of athletes with superior strength endurance, as are sprint cyclists and swimmers. Activities such as jogging, hiking, and skiing can all be enhanced with improved strength endurance.

Strength endurance training and a toning approach are very similar. High reps and short rest periods are suggested. However, depending upon your activity (i.e. distance running, cross-country skiing, etc.), you may wish to perform as many as 40 repetitions per set in your workouts.

Increases in Muscle Power (Explosive Movement) – Power is work x distance / time. Simply stated, muscle power is strength x speed. For example, when you see a 250-pound athlete explode off the floor and travel over ten feet horizontally and three feet vertically to dunk a basketball you are witnessing true muscle power.

Conversely, a 300-pound leg press is not necessarily a good example of power. This is because the speed component is not evident.

Improving power is not as simple as training hard in the weight room. Focused development of explosive movement requires a very specific type of training. The most notable type of power training is plyometrics. The intent of this book is not to detail this type of work.

Plyometric training was pioneered in the old Soviet Union and East Germany. Quite frankly this is one reason their Olympic programs started to soar in the late sixties and early seventies. Plyometric training is designed to "teach" the muscles to respond faster and with more force. This occurs primarily through increases in muscle fiber recruitment and an enhanced response time.

The most common type of plyometric activity involves in-depth, or box jumps. Yet, there are numerous other types of plyometric drills. There are also exercises designed to enhance power in throwing, batting, and racquet sports.

Explosive movement, or power, is obviously crucial to the successful athlete, and resistance training is key to this essential skill. If you continue to be active in your favorite sport(s) while following a sound resistance-training program, your power will improve. On the other hand, if you regularly resistance train, but you are not active in your favorite pastime(s) then you will probably not experience significant gains in power.

Injury Prevention and Rehabilitation – Ask any athletic trainer in the NBA and they will tell you that a good solid strength base will significantly reduce an athletes risk of injury. If an athlete does sustain an injury, the chances are he will recover faster if he has been consistently resistance training. The same is true for everyone who regularly strengthens his or her body. Therefore, if you follow a good resistance training routine your chances of getting injured at work or play are significantly reduced.

In addition to reducing your risk of injury, resistance training is frequently a primary key to rehabilitation from an injury. The knowledgeable sports medicine expert will tell you that strength training is often the primary prescription for the injured athlete. This not only allows the athlete to return to action sooner, it also prepares them better physically for competition.

Better Body Control/Coordination – The added strength, mass and neuromuscular benefits you gain from dumbbell training will aid in your ability to move and function. Not only will you be better prepared for the demands of physical activity; you will be less likely to lose your balance. Sports scientists call this your kinesthetic sense and proprioception. They both refer to your ability to control your body with and without conscious thought. For example, these attributes help determine whether or not you "bust it" after you trip over an obstacle or when you receive and unfriendly shove. As an athlete this translates to a better ability to explosively change direction and a reduction in your risk of injury. In everyday life, improved coordination and body control allows you to function better in all your normal physical activities, from climbing stairs to carrying boxes.

Improved Posture – Good posture not only gives you a more attractive appearance, it also sends a message that you are confident and self-assured. In addition to these attributes, the person with proper posture is able to function better in virtually all of their physical activities. Walking, climbing, jumping running, and resistance training are all enhanced by good posture. This is because body alignment (posture) allows these tasks to be performed with the least amount of stress on the body's joints. A well-developed and well-balanced musculature helps align your body and enhance your posture.

Increased Metabolic Rate – Metabolic rate basically refers to the length of time it takes your body to burn calories. A calorie is a measure for energy (i.e. 1 gram of fat = 9 calories, 1 gram of protein = 4 calories, 1 gram of carbohydrate = 4 calories). The foods you consume supply your body with the fuel that produces the energy for your body to function. These foods are given a caloric value. For example, a McDonald's Big Mac has approximately 590 calories. The caloric break down for a Big Mac is: fat (34g), protein (24g), and carbohydrate (47g). If you consume more calories than you burn then those excess calories are stored as fat.
You will burn calories by resistance training. The energy expenditures associated with this activity can be quite high. The benefits do not stop there, however. The increases in muscle mass you experience through your training will actually increase your resting metabolic rate. This means that you can increase the number of calories you burn even while asleep.

Improved Flexibility – Flexibility typically refers to your ability to move a joint through a complete range of motion without pain. This is a relative term since structurally we all have varying degrees of flexibility potential. Most people have room for improvement when it comes to their ability to demonstrate flexibility. Good flexibility allows you to function with greater ease of movement, and reduces your risk of soft tissue (muscle, tendon, and ligament) damage.
Resistance training can help you improve your flexibility. This is definitely contrary to the old myth that lifters become "muscle bound". Weight lifters are actually one of the most flexible groups of athletes competing in the Olympics. This is because they train through a complete range of motion. This

does not mean that you should start an Olympic lifting program just to improve your flexibility. However, you should train through a complete (pain free) range of motion when you perform resistance exercises. This will allow for a more complete strengthening of the muscle and potentially help your flexibility.

Better Overall Appearance – Although many of us do not like to admit it, our primary motivation for dumbbell training is to improve our appearance. There is no question that a lean and "buff" body is more appealing to the eye than the alternative. This brings us back to a very important note: the only way to completely sculpt your body is via resistance training. Aerobic work by itself will burn calories, but will not stimulate the muscles to grow like resistance training. You can structure your dumbbell training to sculpt your body in different ways (i.e. "toning", bodybuilding, etc.). If you want to pass the mirror test then you must resistance train.

Higher Degree of Self Esteem, Confidence – Strength, hypertrophy, tone, power, strength endurance, injury prevention, power, posture, metabolic rate, flexibility, and appearance are all keys to a high degree of self esteem and confidence. You do not need to be a psychologist to know that the better you feel about yourself the better the quality of your life. You also do not have to be a strength and conditioning expert to understand that dumbbell training is a means to this end.

Dumbbell Training Guidelines

Whether you are a novice or seasoned veteran of resistance training it is a good idea to review and familiarize yourself with sound training guidelines. The rules of training are essential to your success and safety. Please take time to review them and put them into practice.

Medical Checkup – The vast majority of people can exercise safely. However, resistance training may be a health risk to some folks due to a medical problem of which they are unaware. See your doctor and get a thorough checkup prior to beginning a resistance training routine. If you are already physically active and involved in resistance training a medical checkup is still a good idea. NBA players go through a very extensive medical screening prior to each season - and these are some of the most fit athletes in the world. Although it is extremely rare for one of these guys to be excluded from resistance training, there are times when their activities are limited due to medical problems. NBA strength coaches would be unable to properly meet the needs of the player without the information they get from the medical checkup.

Many health care professionals recommend that people over forty and those folks with a history of health problems get a physical exam prior to starting a resistance training program. It is a good idea for you to get a medical checkup regardless of your age.

What to Wear – Workout attire should be safe and comfortable. Street clothes are not recommended, however, as they will be subject to ruin from sweat, and grease and grim from the equipment. Your clothes need to allow freedom of movement without being so loose they can get caught in the equipment. Close-toed shoes are a must. Dropping a weight on an exposed toe can cause major damage, not to mention pain.

Proper Warm-up – It is essential for your safety to warm-up prior to any exercise routine, particularly resistance training. This will help prepare your body for the rigors ahead by increasing your body's blood flow, which in turn increases the muscle core temperature. A warm muscle is more supple and less likely to get hurt. Your warm-up routine should include activities that mimic the type movements you will be doing while exercising. If your going to be weight training we recommend that your warm-up consist of very light sets of the exercises you will be doing. These sets should be done at a 40% to 50% of your 1 repetition maximum for approximately ten repetitions. If you are not sure what this value may be, warm-up with a weight you consider being somewhat non-taxing. For example if you can perform a supine dumbbell press with 40 pounds for ten reps, then warm-up with the 15 to 20 pound dumbbells.

Exercise Technique – Technique is the term used to describe the appropriate physical movements involved in a specific task – in this case resistance-training exercises. You may on occasion hear people use the term "form" interchangeably with technique.

Proper execution of exercise technique is essential for your safety and progress. Make sure you perform each resistance exercise at a speed that allows for complete control (both concentrically and eccentrically) throughout the movement of the drill. This helps eliminate "cheating" or the use of extra body movement as a means of building up momentum in order to complete the task. It is also important that you are familiar with the prescribed movement pattern of the exercise. For example, when performing a supine bench press, the bar should travel in a slight arch. Failure to follow this guideline will place your shoulders in a potentially stressful position and decrease your ability to control the weight.

We also suggest that you train through a full range of motion (ROM) when ever possible. Certain injuries may prevent you from doing this. However, healthy individuals should be able to perform each exercise through a complete ROM. This means that when you weight train you should select a load that can be managed safely through the total movement the exercise.

Breathing – It is a natural tendency to hold your breath during the execution of moderate to heavy lifts. This is called a Valsalva maneuver, and results in an increase of blood pressure and carbon dioxide. This in turn may cause dizziness or fainting.

Some strength and conditioning experts will recommend that you breathe out during the concentric phase of the exercise and inhale during the eccentric. This is good, sound advice, and actually becomes a habit fairly easily.

Balanced Approach – Would you have a contractor build just the front half of your house? Would you ask your mechanic to make sure your cars' tires were out of balance? The answer to these questions is as obvious as the nose on your face – "No!" A half of a house is not very functional, and out of balanced tires cause an uncomfortable ride while possibly creating further problems for your car.

An imbalanced body is like your half a house and out of balanced tires - not too functional. It may appear alright at first glance, but a closer inspection will reveal some glaring deficiencies, and when you try to take it for a spin around the track it is subject to breakdown.

Muscle balance refers to training the biceps relatively equal to that of the triceps, your back equal to your chest, your lower body equal to your upper body, etc. This will help your body function more efficiently, reduce your risk of injury, and enhance your overall appearance.

Progressive Overload – The principle of progressive overload refers to a systematic increase in the demands you place upon your body, and is the basis of all forms of training. You must follow this principle or you will not realize gains in muscle size, strength, or fat loss. When resistance training, you may progress by increasing the number of repetitions you execute in a set, or by increasing the load of a set.

Record Keeping – In the introduction your potential was compared to that of a mountain. Obviously your quest is to reach the top or your peak potential. A log of your journey will let you know just how far you have progressed. Record keeping will also help you follow the principle of progressive overload, as well as assist you in staying organized. It can be quite rewarding, and motivational, to look back at records of past workouts and see how far you have progressed. Included in the back of this book are sample record sheets for your use.

Lifting Accessories – Lifting accessories include items such as gloves, lifting belts, lifting shoes, knee wraps and wrist straps.

Lifting Gloves – The knurling (small ridges to assist your grip) on many bars and dumbbells, and the handles on many weight machines can be quite abrasive. This will make your hands rough and create calluses. Lifting gloves can help prevent this from happening. There are also lifting gloves on the market that may assist in gripping. These gloves usually have a rubber palm with indentations on the surface to help you hold on to the bar.

Lifting gloves typically have open fingers, offering you better finger dexterity. They also usually have a padded and reinforced palm, which can aid in comfort. If you do choose to wear gloves make sure they have a snug fit and allow you to "feel" the weight (for better control).

Lifting Belts are intended to provide you with back support while you lift. It is somewhat debatable as to the amount of support they actually provide. Most experts feel, however, that they do assist in providing additional support for the spinal column during certain lifts (i.e. squats).

Use a belt when performing lifts that create a fair amount of low back stress. Lifts such as squats, dead lifts, cleans, etc. can potentially cause stress on the lower back. On the other hand, we do not recommend that you wear a belt during all of your lifting. This may actually make the muscles that normally assist in lower back support "lazy", because their workload is reduced. If you have a history of lower back problems follow the advice of your doctor. If you currently wear a lifting belt on a regular basis, do not make any sudden or extreme changes in your routine. Gradually reduce the number of belt wearing situations in your workout sessions. This will provide the supporting muscles time to adapt/strengthen.

Lifting Shoes – There are shoes designed for everything nowadays - resistance training included. The lifting shoes on the market are primarily intended for competitive lifters, but are available to anyone willing to spend the money. We recommend a shoe that provides good foot and ankle stability. This eliminates most running shoes. Tennis, basketball, and cross training shoes provide adequate lateral stability and should serve you well in your resistance training.

Knee Wraps – It is not unusual to see competitive lifters (and many recreational lifters) use knee wraps during training and competition. Many lifters feel that wraps provide them with extra support, help alleviate knee pain, and aid in lifting performance. Some experts feel that knee wraps can potentially cause (or contribute to) knee problems such as chondromalacia, which is a roughening behind the kneecap.

Knee wraps should not be confused with knee sleeves. A wrap is usually a cotton elastic blend that comes in a long roll three to six inches in width. It is applied by spiraling and overlapping it up the leg and over the knee. Knee sleeves, on the other hand, are typically elastic or neoprene (a type of dense foam rubber) and slide up the leg and over the knee. They do not supply much additional knee stability unless accompanied by lateral stays.

We do not recommend knee wraps for the average resistance trainer. We also do not encourage the use of knee sleeves unless recommended by a doctor, physical therapists, or certified athletic trainer.

Wrist Straps – Some strength and conditioning coaches call wrist straps, "cheater straps", as they reduce the athlete's requirement on his/her grip strength. Conversely they do allow you to train with heavier weight on exercises like shrugs and power cleans.

Wrist straps are made of cotton or nylon webbing and wrap around your wrist and the bar. This takes stress off of your forearms and makes grip strength less of a factor. The use of them can potentially limit hand flexor strength gains - which may not be in an athlete's best interest.

We think wrist straps are fine for the experienced lifter who is not involved in an activity (or vocation) where grip strength is important. The use of these straps may help you make faster progress in some of your exercises.

CHAPTER 4

Choosing and Organizing a Routine – "A Method to the Madness"

You are undertaking a journey (to your peak physical potential) and need the most efficient and direct route to your destination. You want no detours or delays. You have a desire to get as close to your mountain peak, as fast and as safely as possible. In short, you want a healthier and better-sculpted body, and you want it as soon as possible!

Before beginning your journey, however, there are certain things you need to know. For instance, there are no shortcuts. You may encounter obstacles along the way. Illness and injury, for example, could delay your progress. Perhaps most important you need to determine just where it is you want to go. You must have your destination in mind, before you can map out the best route to get there.

Once you have determined your journey destination (goal) it is important to keep in mind there is more than one way to get there. It may please you to know that some destinations will overlap and you may actually reach more than one goal at a time. You may set out to improve your strength and reduce your body fat percentage at the same time. Do not be surprised to see improved strength endurance accompany better muscle tone. You should expect a reduction in body fat and an increase in your strength if your ultimate goal is to sculpt your body. The by-products of resistance training often go hand in hand and lie close to one another on the mountain.

Goal Specific Training Guidelines "How do you get there from here?"

Before getting down to specifics, it is important to mention a couple of things. First, your body is unique, as is everybody's, and it may not respond to exercise the same as your workout partner. You may burn off fat rapidly while your friend's body takes a bit longer. On the other hand your friend may make strength gains at a faster rate. Secondly, a certain amount of trial and error will be necessary when establishing your resistance training program. For example, you may find that one type of approach is providing you with great strength gains but not the "sculpting " response you were looking for. Keep these points in mind when following the program you select. Yet, you should know that the guidelines provided are not based on guesswork. They are established as a result of years of research and observation by resistance training experts. So, take this information and "tweak" your approach occasionally if you see the need.

Strength Training

How many days a week?	3 to 4
How many sets per exercise?	2 to 5
How many repetitions per set?	2 to 8 (4 to 6 most often)
How long a rest period between sets?	1 to 3 minutes

Additional notes: You may wish to do a total body approach 3 days a week (i.e. M-W-F). You may choose to split your routine over four days (i.e. M,T,TH,F) working upper body one day and lower body the next. Power lifters seem to prefer a 4 day a week approach. In order to make optimal gains it is important to have variety in your lifting program

Body Building

How many days a week?	3 to 6
How many sets per exercise?	2 to 5
How many sets per body part?	6 to 12
How many repetitions per set?	8 to 16 (10 to 12 most often)
How long a rest period between sets?	a few seconds to 2 minutes

Additional notes: Body Builders typically follow a "split routine". They will train one to three body parts per work out session. A common approach is 3 days on and 1 or 2 day(s) off. Workout days are often divided into exercises targeting chest and triceps one day, back and biceps the next and legs and shoulders on the third day. Yet, you may feel more comfortable with a different split (i.e. chest and back, arms and shoulders, legs and low back).

"Toning"

How many days a week?	2 to 3
How many sets per exercise?	1 to 3
How many repetitions per set?	10 to 20
How long a rest period between sets?	Less than 1 minute

Additional notes: The desired results here are a little muscle hypertrophy, strength (endurance) gains, and reduced body fat. Short rest periods between sets are essential for toning success. For the best results you should incorporate an aerobic training (jogging, cycling, aerobics, etc.) regime into your weekly routine.

Muscle Power (Explosive Movement)

How many days a week?	3 to 4
How many sets per exercise?	2 to 5
How many repetitions per set?	2 to 8 (4 to 6 most often)
How long a rest period between sets?	2 to 3 minutes

Additional notes: To improve explosive movement, it is very important to raise your level of strength. You may wish to incorporate Olympic-type lifts into your training regime. Many experts feel that this is an excellent approach to enhanced power because it includes a speed component. The best approach to improving power is a sound strength training routine accompanied by plyometric training. Plyometrics are the best tool for combining the speed and strength components of power.

Body Control

How many days a week?	2 to 6
How many sets per exercise?	2 to 5
How many repetitions per set?	6 to 20
How long a rest period between sets?	a few seconds to 2 minutes

Additional notes: Body control training can be quite beneficial to everyone, but it is essential for the athlete. This type of training can be combined with a strength training, toning, bodybuilding or power development approach. The key is the use of dumbbells and the addition of an "unstable" physical environment. For example, performing dumbbell curls while standing on a balance board.

NOTE: Extra caution should be used when performing these exercises due to the unstable environment in which they are performed.

Various Training Routines and Approaches "Maps to Your Peak"

There are numerous approaches to resistance training which are designed to meet different goals. The training routine you select should offer variety and be conducive to helping you reach your goals. For example, circuit training is a good approach for toning, but not necessarily for strength training. It is important to note that as you advance in your training you may choose to combine or overlap various training routines.

The Delorme Approach

This approach is perhaps the most common resistance training routine. Although it is not always referred by its correct name. In the 1950s, T.L. Delorme introduced a training system based on 3 sets of 10 repetitions. Set one is to be performed at 50% of your 10 RM. Set 2 is a set of 75% of your 10 RM and the third set is 100% of your 10 RM. For example, if you can lift 100 pounds 10 times (but no more than 10) while performing the bench press, you have 10 RM of 100 pounds. In this situation your first set would be 50 pounds for 10 repetitions (50 lbs x 10 reps); your second set, 75 pounds for 10 repetitions (75 lbs x 10 reps); and your third set, 100 pounds for 10 repetitions (100 lbs x 10 reps). This is a great workout for beginners, no matter what their fitness goal may be.

Periodization (Cycling)

A periodized approach typically entails a mapped out plan that covers 12 to 16 weeks. Most periodized programs consist of three cycles or phases. The idea behind this type of approach is to help you reach your strength peak at the end of 10 to 16 week period.

Phase one is the base period in which you acclimate your body to resistance training, as well as building a strength endurance base. High repetitions, and short rest periods between sets of one to one and a half minutes mark this cycle. Phase two is a bit more conducive to strength gains and less likely to help strength endurance (dependent upon your repetitions per exercise). It consists of fewer reps per set than cycle one and has rest periods of approximately two minutes between sets. Phase three is the peak phase and will help you produce your best strength output. Low reps, high weight, and long rest periods between sets mark this cycle. At the end of the last phase a period of "active rest" lasting a few days to a week is observed before starting the program over again at phase one. No resistance training should take place during the active rest phase. You should not become a couch potato, either. Use this time to do some light enjoyable activities, such as cycling, hiking, etc. A periodized approach can be altered to offer mini cycles of one day to two weeks each. The ultimate goal of increased strength is still there.

The key to a periodization system is the structured approach that forces you to vary your workout. This is the most popular approach to strength training in college and professional athletics. This may be the best system for folks with a primary goal of improved strength and power. However, this approach can be altered to meet the needs of the body builder or the person who wishes to tone their muscles.

Sample Periodization Routine (for Strength Gains)

Phase I (4 weeks)
(1 to 1.5 mins. rest between sets)

(Monday)

Exercise	Sets	Repetitions
Chest Press	4	10-12 RM
Pullover	4	10-12 RM
Shoulder Press	3	10-12 RM
Squats	4	10-12 RM
Rumanian Dead Lifts	4	10-12 RM
Heel Raises	4	20-24 RM

(Wednesday)

Exercise	Sets	Repetitions
Incline Press	4	10-12 RM
Dumbbell Row	4	10-12 RM
Shoulder Flies	3	10-12 RM
Lunge	4	10-12 RM
Single Leg Dead Lifter	4	10-12 RM
Heel Raises	4	20-24 RM

(Friday)

Exercise	Sets	Repetitions
Chest Press	4	10-12 RM
Pullover	4	10-12 RM
Shoulder Press	3	10-12 RM
Squats	4	10-12 RM
Rumanian Dead Lifts	4	10-12 RM
Heel Raises	4	20-24 RM

Phase II (4 weeks)
(2 minutes rest between sets)

(Monday)

Exercise	Sets	Repetitions	
Chest Press	4	7-9	RM
Pullover	4	7-9	RM
Shoulder Press	3	7-9	RM
Squats	4	7-9	RM
Dead Lifts	4	7-9	RM
Heel Raises	4	18-20 RM	

(Wednesday)

Exercise	Sets	Repetitions	
Incline Press	4	7-9	RM
Dumbbell Row	4	7-9	RM
Shoulder Flies	3	7-9	RM
Lunge	4	7-9	RM
Single Leg Dead Lifter	4	7-9	RM
Heel Raises	4	18-20 RM	

(Friday)

Exercise	Sets	Repetitions	
Chest Press	4	7-9	RM
Pullover	4	7-9	RM
Shoulder Press	3	7-9	RM
Squats	4	7-9	RM
Dead Lifts	4	7-9	RM
Heel Raises	4	18-20 RM	

Phase III (4 weeks)
(2.5 to 3 minutes rest between sets)

(Monday)

Exercise	Sets	Repetitions	
Chest Press	4	4-6	RM
Pullover	4	4-6	RM
Shoulder Press	3	4-6	RM
Squats	4	4-6	RM
Dead Lifts	4	4-6	RM
Heel Raises	4	18-20	RM

(Wednesday)

Exercise	Sets	Repetitions	
Incline Press	4	4-6	RM
Dumbbell Row	4	4-6	RM
Shoulder Flies	3	4-6	RM
Lunge	4	4-6	RM
Single Leg Dead Lifter	4	4-6	RM
Heel Raises	4	18-20	RM

(Friday)

Exercise	Sets	Repetitions	
Chest Press	4	4-6	RM
Pullover	4	4-6	RM
Shoulder Press	3	4-6	RM
Squats	4	4-6	RM
Dead Lifts	4	4-6	RM
Heel Raises	4	18-20	RM

NOTE: By altering the rest periods, exercises, and repetitions this routine could easily be designed to meet the needs of the body builder.

Pyramid Routine

The pyramid system is one of the more common approaches to resistance training. This routine typically entails 4 to 6 sets of the same exercise. The sets progress from low weight and high repetitions to high weight and low repetitions. This approach can be extended, allowing you to work your way back down to lighter weights and higher repetitions.

Each pyramid session offers variety, and can prove effective in producing gains in strength and muscle hypertrophy. This is a very common chest press workout, but it can be used with any lifting exercise. This system is recommended for the body builder, athlete and strength trainer. It is possible to tailor this approach to accommodate those interested in toning, although it is not the most ideal routine for that particular goal.

Sample Pyramid Routine (Chest Press)

Set #	# of Repetitions	Weight (lbs)
1	12	20
2	10	30
3	8	40
4	6	50
5	4	60
6	2	70

Single Set to "Muscle Failure"

The manufacturers of Nautilus exercise equipment in the 1970s and 80s popularized the single set to "muscle failure". The term "muscle failure" is misleading, as this is not what happens during the execution of this approach. In fact, the muscles become fatigued to the point they can no longer apply the force to move the resistance. They do not "fail".

This system of training is marked by 1 set of eight to 12 repetitions (although various repetition frames are often prescribed). The idea is that you find a weight that you can lift for eight repetitions. Once you progress (over a period of lifting sessions) to the point that you can perform 12 repetitions then the load should be increased.

This approach can produce gains in strength and muscle hypertrophy. However, a multiple set system will most likely provide better results. On the other hand, single set training sessions do not require much time to complete.

The single set system is very good for the beginner and those folks interested in toning. We also recommend this approach to people with very limited time in which to train. We do not recommend this approach to the serious strength trainer, athlete, or body builder.

Circuit Training

Circuit training is an approach based on the use of a series of exercise stations that you progress through. Each set is based on either a specific number of repetitions (i.e. 10 - 12) or a given time period (i.e. 30 seconds). Circuit training is typically a machine type workout, but this is not a necessity, as dumbbells, pushups, abdominal work, dips, etc. can easily be incorporated. This system is ideal for the person with limited time and it is the approach recommended first for folks interested in toning (with reps of 16 plus), and for the beginner

Station #1	Station #2	Station #3	Station #4
Chest Press	Pullover	Shoulder Press	Biceps Curls
Station #5	Station #6	Station #7	Station #8
Triceps Ext.	Dumbbell Rows	Chest Flies	Crunches
Station #9	Station #10	Station #11	Station #12
Sumo Squat	Lunge	Rumanian Dead Lifts	Heel Raises

Power Lifting

Power lifting is a competitive sport that entails demonstrations of strength through maximum lifts in the bench press, dead lift, and squat. Power lifters typically train with heavy weight, and with repetitions of six and less. It is not uncommon for a power lifter to follow a periodization approach.

Although they compete in only the three lifts, their training routine includes multiple complimentary exercises. For example, a training session may include dumbbell presses and incline bench to help enhance bench press performance.

Body builders will often use a power lifting approach during certain times of the year in order to increase their strength. In the long run, this will actually help them increase muscle size, as well as their capacity for work.

A power lifting approach is recommended for many athletes, body builders, and strength trainers. Some strength and conditioning coaches feel that a power lifting approach is absolutely necessary for the athlete. On the other hand, there are numerous routes to improving athletic performance and this is just one approach. This system is also bit advanced for the beginner. A period of muscular adaptation through a more conservative system (i.e. circuit training) is recommended before undertaking a power lifting routine.

Olympic Lifting

Like power lifting, Olympic lifting is advanced in nature and also a competitive sport. Olympic lifters compete in two lifts, the clean and jerk and the snatch. The proper execution of these two lifts requires a great deal of technique, and is not easily learned.

Ironically, there is a much larger power component involved in Olympic style lifting than in power lifting. This is because speed of movement is a major key to the execution of an Olympic lift.

Olympic style lifting is ideal for many athletes, and can easily be adapted to dumbbells. The power component of these exercises complements the explosive movement involved in many sports. As a result, coaches will often have their players perform variations of the Olympic lifts. Power cleans, hang cleans and push presses are examples of these supplemental exercises.

There is a high risk of injury when any of these lifts are performed with poor technique. For this reason we do not recommend this system for most people. If you are interested in Olympic lifting it is essential that you learn proper execution from a qualified strength and conditioning specialist. Body builders, power lifters, weekend warriors and body sculptors of all types would be well advised not to pursue Olympic style lifting unless they have plans to compete in this sport.

Super Sets

Body builders often use super sets, but they could also help the person interested in toning. Super sets are performed by executing two (sometimes more) different exercises in rapid succession. This is usually done with exercises of opposing muscle groups (i.e. chest and back), but can be done with exercises targeting the same muscle group. For example, on a chest day you may super set dumbbell chest flies with flat dumbbell chest presses.

You may choose to incorporate super sets at the end of a normal workout. This will help insure an intense training session. This routine can also serve you well on days in which your workout time is limited, as you can make your entire session super sets. Due to the short rest periods, the super set system is also an excellent tool for those people interested in enhancing strength endurance.

Note: A common believe among strength and conditioning professionals is that a high repetition and short rest period approach is most conducive to gains in muscle hypertrophy. There is research that supports this believe. Also supporting this line of thought is the feedback furnished by successful body builders. Based on this information, super sets are for body builders, toners and endurance athletes (i.e. distance runners). The repetition frame (# of repetitions per set) can be manipulated to help meet your needs.

Drop Sets (Burn outs)

Drop sets are typically done on the last set of an exercise. They are executed by rapidly reducing the weight of an exercise and continuing with more repetitions. This is continued for four to six more successive sets. Drop sets are more conveniently performed on a programable machine, but can easily be managed with dumbbells. A reduction of 10 to 20 pounds per set will allow you to continue with an easy and safe progression. You should always do drop sets with the assistance of a spotter.

Drop sets are recommended for body builders and body toners. This is also one of the better approaches for the endurance trainer (athlete). Like super sets, the rep frame is easily manipulated to accommodate your needs.

Forced Reps

Forced reps require the assistance of an experienced spotter and are typically performed on the last set of an exercise. Upon the completion of your last repetition (the last you can do on your own), your partner assists you in lifting the load one to five more times. Help is only provided on the concentric (positive) part of the lift, but the spotter remains ready to assist if necessary during the eccentric (negative) phase.

The training benefits to forced reps are similar in nature to that of a burnout session. Therefore, this type of routine would make a good occasional training session for the body builder, toner, and endurance athlete.

Negatives (Eccentric Training)

Be prepared for a lot of muscle soreness if you take on a negative training session. This lifting approach can be managed in two ways. The first approach is like a forced rep with additional weight (via force applied from your partner) added during the eccentric (negative) phase of the lift. You will obviously need assistance on the concentric (positive) phase of the exercise (as we mentioned earlier, you are able to control the descent of significantly more weight than you can lift). The other approach entails additional resistance added on every repetition of the set. Initially help is not necessary during the concentric phase, but will be in short order.

There is research that suggests eccentric work is necessary for muscle hypertrophy gains. There are also studies that suggest strength gains come about faster via programs that provide eccentric work as opposed to those that do not (for example, certain machines provide little or no eccentric work). Some experts figure it stands to reason that additional negative resistance would produce greater gains in strength and muscle size. Incorporate negative work into your routine occasionally – once a week, max. The soreness associated with this type training can be quite significant, so plan accordingly before undertaking eccentric training. Safety should be your major concern with this style approach. Therefore, only experienced lifters with experienced partners should attempt this routine.

Split Routine

As mentioned earlier, body builders, power lifters, and many recreational resistance trainers will split up their lifting routine. For example, a power lifter and athlete may choose to do a four day split, doing upper body exercises two days of the week and lower body exercises on the other two. Body builders and other body sculptors often split their routines to work specific body parts (i.e. chest & back, arms & shoulders, legs & trunk) on different days.

Other systems may be used within the split routine. For example, you may choose to do drop sets on your chest and triceps day, forced reps on your back and biceps day, and super sets on your leg and shoulder day.

Sample Split Routine

Day	Body Parts	Sets Each Part	Reps	Rest Period
Mon.	Chest/Triceps	12/7	10-12	1 Min.
Tues.	Legs/Shoulders	16/8	12-14/10-12	1 Min
Wed.	Back/Biceps	12/7	10-12	1 Min.
Thurs.	Rest or Cardio/Abs (no resistance training)			
Friday	Chest Triceps	12/7	10-12	1 Min.
Sat.	Legs/Shoulders	16/8	12-14/10-12	1 Min.
Sun.	Backs/Biceps	12/7	10-12	1 Min.
Mon.	Rest or Cardio/Abs (no resistance training)			

Body Control Training

Body control training is quite unique and on the cutting edge of physical development. We will discuss exercises for this system in greater detail in chapter 11.

Basic resistance training usually helps you move about with a greater ease. This is a result of improved strength and coordination. Body control training takes coordination and movement development another giant step forward. This type of system combines resistance training with balance (proprioceptive, kinesthetic awareness) development.
    Body control training entails resistance exercises that are performed in a non-stable environment. For example, instead of regular flat dumbbell presses, you would do an alternating dumbbell press with your feet up and off the floor. This makes it necessary for the muscles in your trunk to become involved in order to avoid falling off the bench. Initially this task will seem quite difficult, but as your body adapts it will become easier. Another example of body control training includes exercises performed on a balance, or wobble board. The idea is that your body constantly seeks to find the balance point while performing various lifts (i.e. dumbbell curls, triceps kickbacks, lateral flies, etc.)

The benefits of body control training include an enhanced ability to function in your daily activities, whether climbing stairs, moving from one part of the office to another, or sprinting down the basketball court. Many experts feel that demonstrations of strength will be enhanced as a result of neuromuscular gains associated with body control training. For example, if you want to increase your bench press the alternating dumbbell press with your feet up would be a great supplemental exercise.

Body control training is very advanced in nature, and is not suggested for beginners. It is however, highly recommended for body builders, strength trainers and athletes in particular.

CHAPTER 5
Chest Exercises
Dumbbell Supine Bench Press

Primary muscles targeted and developed: Pectoralis major, Anterior deltoid, Triceps.

Technique: Start with your back flat on the bench and your feet flat on the floor with the dumbbells securely grasped in each hand. The dumbbells should be situated so that the head of the dumbbell is touching the side of your chest. Raise the dumbbells in a slight arch (not as great an arch as in the barbell bench) and lightly touch the dumbbell heads once your arms are fully extended. Lower the dumbbells in a very slow controlled manner (4 second count) and repeat.

Precautions: The total weight you use during a dumbbell press should be lighter than that of a barbell bench, because the dumbbells are more difficult to control. Use caution lifting the dumbbells into the starting position as they can shift and cause potential injury (particular to the shoulders). When lowering the dumbbells to the floor use care not to drop them as this may cause injury

to yourself and/or others around you. Dropping the dumbbells may also result in breaking the equipment. Make sure the area around you is clear of other dumbbells and clutter. [We witnessed a guy crush his fingers when he dropped his dumbbells and one landed on top of another one (that his partner had negligently left out) with his hand still firmly attached to the handle.] Always use a spotter.

Spotting: It is suggested that your spotter be prepared to grab your wrists when assisting. Some experts suggest that the spotter assist at the elbows. This is somewhat risky as it does not adequately protect the shoulders and elbows. You may wish to use two spotters – one on either side. This will allow them to hand you the dumbbells at a safe beginning position as well as assist you in lowering the dumbbells when finished.

Notes: The dumbbell press is an excellent supplement or alternative to the barbell bench press. We often recommend this lift to athletes and body builders as it helps ensure equal development between right and left sides. The dumbbell press also helps develop the muscles that support the shoulders and elbows, thus potentially enhancing performance (on the court, field, or weight room) and reducing risk of injury.

Incline Dumbbell Press

Primary muscles targeted and developed: (Upper) Pectoralis major, Anterior deltoid, Triceps

Technique: Same as incline barbell bench, except dumbbells start at a deeper position.

Precautions: Same as flat dumbbell press.

Spotting: Same as flat dumbbell press.

Notes: The incline dumbbell press may be the best exercise for developing the upper chest. This is supported by research that indicates that more of the muscle fibers of the upper pec come into play when performing this exercise than do when performing the incline barbell press.

Decline Dumbbell Press

Primary muscles targeted and developed: Pectoralis major, Anterior deltoid, Triceps.

Technique: Same as flat bench except the bar is lowered to the lower chest area at the bottom of sternum.

Precautions: Same as flat bench press. Extra caution should be taken if you have a shoulder injury or have experienced shoulder problems in the past.

Spotting: Same as flat bench press.

Notes: This chest exercise places a greater emphasis on the lower pecs. This exercise is not essential for strength trainers or athletes, but it can be a good supplemental lift. We do feel that body builders should include this exercise in their training routine.

Dumbbell Flies

Primary muscles targeted and developed: Pectoralis major, Anterior deltoids.

Technique: Start with your back flat on the bench and your feet flat on the floor. Grasp dumbbells firmly in each hand and extend arms so that the dumbbells are touching immediately above the chest. Slightly bend your elbows and lower the dumbbells toward the floor in a very slow controlled manner (4 second count) and repeat. Lower the weight until the dumbbells are slightly lower than the top of your chest. Your elbows should remain locked at the same angle throughout this exercise. It may help in execution to imagine yourself hugging a large tree – this exercise is sometimes referred to as tree huggers.

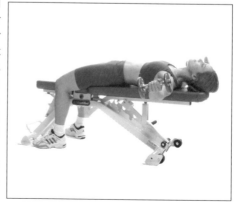

Precautions: This exercise can be very stressful to the shoulder.

People with a history of shoulder problems should avoid this lift. Always use a spotter when performing this exercise.

Spotting: We suggest that your spotter be prepared to grab your wrists when assisting.

Notes: The dumbbell fly targets development of the pecs. We often recommend this lift to athletes and body builders as it helps insure equal development between right and left sides. The dumbbell fly also helps develop the muscles that support the shoulders and elbows, thus potentially enhancing performance (on the court, field, or weight room) and reducing risk of injury. This exercise can be done in a supine decline or incline position.

Chapter 6
Back Exercises

Dumbbell Row

Primary muscles targeted and developed: Latissimus dorsi, Trapezius, Posterior deltoids, Rhomboids, and Biceps.

Technique: When working your right side, place your left knee and left hand (with arm fully extended) on a flat bench. (This will help you maintain a safe low back position.) Firmly grasp the dumbbell with your right hand and lift the weight straight up until it touches your chest. A slight rotation of the trunk is acceptable. Lower the dumbbell in a slow (4 second count) controlled manner until your arm is fully extended. Do not allow the dumbbell to touch the floor between repetitions.

Precautions: Although this lift is more "back friendly" than the barbell row people with low back pain and problems may still wish to avoid it. It is essential that you not jerk the weight up with your lower back and that you refrain from excessive twisting type movements when performing this lift.

Spotting: It is not essential to use a spotter during this exercise.

Notes: This is a great exercise for developing the back (middle and upper). This lift is recommended for strength trainers, athletes, and body builders

Shrugs

Primary muscles targeted and developed: Trapezius.

Technique: Firmly grasp dumbbells. Keep your arms fully extended. Raise the weight by shrugging your shoulders (your elbows should not bend). This movement is much like the one you may do when you respond in the negative, non-verbally, to a question. A bewildered look on your face is optional during the execution of this lift. Try to touch your ears with your shoulders while "tucking" your chin to your chest. Your movements should be slow and controlled (3 to 4 seconds on the positive and negative).

Precautions: Take care in lifting the weights to initiate this lift - particularly if you are lifting the weight off the floor. In this case follow sound lifting principles and bend your knees, keep your back straight and keep the weight located close to your body. Lift the weight with your legs, not your back.

Spotting: Spotters are generally not necessary for this lift.

Notes: This exercise targets the upper back. It is the best exercise available for developing the upper regions of the trapezius. This exercise is recommended for athletes, strength trainers, body builders, and toners.

Dual Dumbbell Pullover (with Crunch)

Primary muscles targeted and developed: Pectoralis major, Latissimus dorsi, Hip Flexors, and Abdominals.

Technique: Start with your back flat on the bench and your legs fully extended with your heels on the floor. Hold dumbbells in each hand with a neutral grip. "Hang" them behind your head toward the floor. Lock your elbows at a 90-degree angle. Simultaneously lift your legs, until they are vertical to the floor, and pull the dumbbells over until they are above your chest. Slowly (4-second count) lower them together, but allow neither to touch the floor. Repeat the same movement pattern.

Precautions: Shoulder injuries / problems may preclude you from executing this exercise. Also, due to the leg lift, your pelvis will experience a big forward tilt - for this reason this is not a back friendly exercise. If you have back problems or if your back feels uncomfortable during this exercise it may be in your best interest to avoid, or eliminate the leg lift portion.

Spotting: Spotters are not necessary for this lift.

Notes: You can alter this exercise by using a single dumbbell for the pullover. Using two dumbbells helps ensure equal development of the right and left sides of your body. You may wish to eliminate the leg lift portion if you have lower back problems, or if you are just learning this exercise.

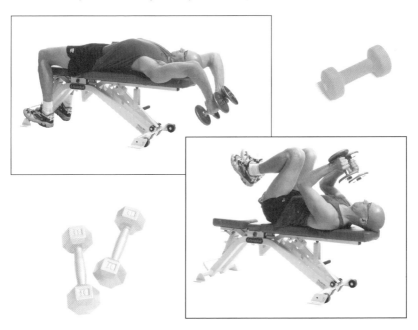

Bentover Flies

Primary muscles targeted and developed: Trapezius, Latissimus dorsi, and Rhomboids

Technique: Start with your legs slightly flexed and your feet slightly wider than shoulder width apart. Bend at the waist so that your back is almost parallel to the floor. Hold your shoulders back and keep your head up. This will help you maintain good posture throughout the lift. Hold dumbbells in each hand with a neutral grip. "Hang" them toward the floor. Slightly flex your elbows and raise the dumbbells until they are at the same level as your shoulders. Slowly (4 second count) lower them together. Repeat the same movement pattern.

Precautions: Shoulder and low back injuries / problems may preclude you from executing this exercise.

Spotting: Spotters are not necessary for this lift, but can be used to assist in negative or forced rep training.

Notes: You can alter this exercise by performing it with your chest on a incline bench or stability ball.

CHAPTER 7
Shoulder Exercises

Arnold's

Primary muscles targeted and developed: Deltoids, Trapezius, and Triceps.

Technique: This exercise can be done seated or standing. With both approaches care should be taken to keep your body erect with good posture. The starting position and the initial upward movement of this exercise are what distinguish it from a regular dumbbell shoulder press. You should grasp the dumbbells firmly and hold them at chest level with your palms facing in. Lift the weight and turn your palms out simultaneously until your arms are fully extended. At the peak of the lift your palms should be facing out. The dumbbell heads should be touching at the start of each rep and again (the opposite heads this time) at the end of each rep. Movements should be controlled and the weights lowered on a four-second count.

Precautions: The same shoulder and back (posture) precautions should be taken with this lift as are taken with the shoulder press.

Spotting: It is necessary to have a spotter throughout the execution of this exercise. The spotter should be prepared to grab the lifter's wrist (as opposed to the elbows) if help is needed.

Notes: This exercise will incorporate help from the pectoralis as well as other supporting muscles around the shoulder. We recommend this exercise for athletes, strength trainers, body builders, and toners.

Lateral Dumbbell Raise (Fly)

Primary muscles targeted and developed: Deltoids, Trapezius.

Technique: While standing with good posture, grasp the dumbbells with your elbows slightly bent. Hold them so that they are resting on the front of your thighs. (The grip you are to use is called a neutral grip. This means that the palms of your hands are facing each other and not facing out or in toward your body.) Raise the dumbbells until they are level with your ears. Lower them on a four-second count until they are in front of your thighs again.

Precautions: This exercise is considerable more shoulder friendly than any of the overhead lifts. However, folks with shoulder problems may be well advised to avoid this lift or to train with very light weight. You should also make a conscious effort to keep good posture and not propel the dumbbells up by swinging your back.

Spotting: A spotter is not necessary with this lift. However, you may decide to use a spotter for forced reps, or for advanced lifters, and negatives.

Notes: This is a super shoulder exercise. Recommended for athletes, strength trainers, body builders, and toners.

Upright Row

Primary muscles targeted and developed: Deltoids, Trapezius.

Technique: Grasp the dumbbells so that the heads are touching and the weights themselves are resting on your upper thighs. Your feet should be shoulder width apart and your arms should be fully extended. With your body erect, pull the dumbbells up, keeping them within inches of your abdomen and chest, until they are level with your clavicle. Your elbows should be higher than your ears at the lifts highest point. Lower the dumbbells in a slow (4 second count) controlled manner and repeat.

Precautions: This exercise is more shoulder friendly than most overhead lifts, but it is still not recommended for people with shoulder problems. Also, poor lifting technique could injure your low back. Good posture and strict attention to lifting protocol is a must. It is important to avoid propelling the dumbbells up with a low back swing and to keep them close to your body throughout the lift.

Spotting: A spotter is not essential for this lift. However, you can use a spotter to assist with forced reps, or with advanced lifters, and negatives.

Notes: This lift is an important teaching tool for the potential Olympic lifter. Under proper supervision explosive variations of this exercise can be incorporated. Recommended for athletes, strength trainers, and body builders.

Frontal Dumbbell Raise

Primary muscles targeted and developed: (frontal) Deltoids, (upper) Pectoralis major.

Technique: While standing with good posture, grasp (palms facing in) the dumbbells with your elbows slightly bent. Hold them so that they are resting on the front of your thighs. Raise the dumbbells straight in front of you (at a shoulder's width) until they are level with your ears. Lower them on a four-second count until they are in front of your thighs again. Repeat.

Precautions: This exercise is considerably more shoulder friendly than any of the over head lifts. However, folks with shoulder problems may be well advised to avoid this lift or to train with very light weight. You should also make a conscious effort to keep good posture and not propel the dumbbells up by swinging your back.

Spotting: A spotter is not necessary with this lift. However, you may decide to use a spotter for forced reps, or with advanced lifters, negatives.

Notes: This is a very good shoulder exercise. Recommended for athletes, strength trainers, body builders, and toner

Four Way Shoulder

Primary muscles targeted and developed: Deltoids (anterior, posterior, and medial), Trapezius, Rhomboids, and Latisimus dorsi.

Technique: This is a four-part exercise that targets the entire shoulder area – Bent-over Flies, Lateral Flies, 35-Degree Flies, and Frontal Flies. Other than the Bent-over Fly portion of the lift, each section should be performed with the thumbs pointing up. Follow the procedure for Bent-over Flies and execute 11 reps. Go directly from this segment to the Lateral Flies, and perform 11 more reps, while following proper technique with thumbs (thus dumbbell heads) pointing up. Advance immediately from this part to the 35 Degree fly by moving your arms slightly (approximately 35 degrees) toward your body's mid point. Finish this routine with 11 thumb-up Frontal Flies. Each segment should be performed with your body in good alignment and posture. Lift the dumbbells until they are level with your ears on each rep of each part of this routine. Raise and lower them on a four-second count. Repeat each movement until a segment is complete then immediately advance to the next.

Precautions: This exercise is considerably more shoulder friendly than any of the over head lifts. However, folks with shoulder problems may be well advised to avoid this lift or to train with very light weight. You should also make a conscious effort to keep good posture and not propel the dumbbells up by swinging your back.

Spotting: A spotter is not necessary with this lift.

Notes: This is a very good shoulder exercise, and should be incorporated prior to starting most upper body lifting sessions. This will serve as a great warm-up and injury prevention routine. Recommended for athletes, strength trainers, body builders, and toners. Training weight should range from nothing more than arm weight itself, to seven pounds. Two to five pound dumbbells are the norm.

Chapter 8
Arm Exercises

Dumbbell Curls

Primary muscles targeted and developed: Biceps brachii, Brachialis, and Brachioradialis.

Technique: Stand with your feet shoulder width apart and your knees slightly bent. Grasp the dumbbells firmly and let your arms hang by your side. Bring the dumbbells up by bending (flexing) your arms at the elbow. Rotate your hands so that at the bottom of the lift you have a neutral grip and at the top your palms are facing in. Your elbows should remain locked at your side. Raise the dumbbells until they are just a few inches away from your deltoids. Do not let the dumbbells "rest" at the height of the lift. Lower the dumbbells on a four-second count until arms are fully extended.

Precautions: Do not swing your back in order to propel the dumbbells up. Folks with back problems may wish to do this exercise seated. This will help eliminate excess movement of the low back. Elbow problems (i.e. tennis elbow or elbow tendonitis) may preclude you from doing this exercise.

Spotting: A spotter is not necessary for this lift. However you may wish to use a spotter to assist with forced reps or negative training.

Notes: This is probably the second most (to the flat bench press) popular lift in the U.S. This goes back to the mirror check – you notice your biceps and pectoralis first and most often. Do not place an over emphasis on this lift. On the other hand, if you are an athlete or strength trainer do not fall into the "biceps ain't important" trap preached by some coaches. The bottom-line, develop your biceps proportionate to the other parts of your body. For example, they are a relatively small muscle group and should not be trained as much as your chest or back. Recommended for body builders, toners, athletes and strength trainers.

Additional Note: To target different parts of the biceps you may wish to incorporate "preacher curls" and incline curls. A "preacher curl" is

performed on a seated bench that has an angled pad for support of your upper arms. When performing this curl you start with a small contraction of the biceps (its origin is in the shoulder area) due to the angle of your arm. An incline curl is done while lying back on a bench at a 45 degree angle. This exercise starts with a pre-stretch of the biceps.

Due to the different angles of these two lifts, your body recruits muscle fibers from different areas of the biceps to complete the task. This in turn allows for a more complete development of the muscle.

Dumbbell Concentration Curls

Primary muscles targeted and developed: Biceps brachii, Brachialis, and Brachioradialis.

Technique: Sit on the end of a bench with your feet flat on the floor, and greater than shoulder width apart. Grasp one dumbbell firmly and let your arm hang. Bend at your waist so that your elbow is making contact with the inside of your thigh. Bring the dumbbell up by bending (flexing) your arm at the elbow (do not allow your leg to move or shift). Rotate your hands so that at the bottom of the lift you have a neutral grip and at the top your palms are facing in. Your elbow should remain locked on the inside of your thigh. Do not let the dumbbell "rest" at the height of the lift. Lower the dumbbell on a four-second count until arms are fully extended. Work each arm equally following the same technique for each.

Precautions: Do not lift your back, or move your leg in order to propel the dumbbell up. Elbow problems (i.e. tennis elbow or elbow tendonitis) may preclude you from doing this exercise.

Spotting: A spotter is not necessary for this lift. However you may wish to use a spotter to assist with forced reps or negative training.

Notes: Recommended for body builders, toners, athletes and strength trainers.

Hammer Curls

Primary muscles targeted and developed: Biceps brachii, Brachialis, and Brachioradialis.

Technique: Stand with your feet shoulder width apart and your knees slightly bent. Grasp the dumbbells firmly and let your arms hang by your side. Bring the dumbbells up by bending (flexing) your arms at the elbow. Keep your hands in the neutral grip throughout this lift (so do not rotate your hands). Your elbows should remain locked at your side. Raise the dumbbells until they are just a few inches away from your deltoids. Do not let the dumbbells "rest" at the height of the lift. Lower the dumbbells on a four-second count until arms are fully extended.

Precautions: Do not swing your back in order to propel the dumbbells up. Folks with back problems may wish to do this exercise seated. This will help eliminate excess movement of the lower back. Elbow problems (i.e. tennis elbow or elbow tendonitis) may preclude you from doing this exercise.

Spotting: A spotter is not necessary for this lift. However you may wish to use a spotter to assist with forced reps or negative training.

Notes: This exercise (along with incline curls) is ideal for targeting the Brachialis. This a relatively large muscle located under the Biceps brachii. Recommended for athletes, strength trainers, body builders, and toners.

Dumbbell Triceps Extensions

Primary muscles targeted and developed: Triceps.

Technique: Stand with your feet shoulder width apart and your knees slightly bent. Grasp a dumbbell in one hand and hold it above your head with the elbow of that arm pointing up. Secure that arm by grasping it with the opposite hand around the triceps area. Start with your elbow bent and the dumbbell behind your head. Lift the weight by extending your elbow fully. Lock your arm in place (with the help of your other arm) and keep your elbow pointing up throughout this exercise. Lower the dumbbell slowly on a four-second count.

Precautions: Lifting your arm above your head to execute this exercise may aggravate your shoulder if you have a pre existing shoulder problem. Folks with elbow tendonitis or other problems may wish to avoid this lift. Take care not to hit yourself in the head with the dumbbell when doing this exercise. (Don't laugh, we have seen this happen before.)

Spotting: A spotter is necessary if you are attempting this exercise with heavy weight. The spotter should stand behind you and have their hands matched up with the dumbbell heads. If a problem arises they can then quickly grab the dumbbell.

Notes: This exercise can be performed with both arms and a heavier dumbbell. When doing this exercise with both arms, make a conscious effort to keep your elbows in tight and to not let them "flair" out.

You will train your triceps quite a bit when you resistance train without targeting them. For example, when you bench press, shoulder press, or even do pushups, your triceps do a lot of work. Use good judgment when training your triceps - do not over work them. Train them proportionate to your biceps. You do six sets of biceps exercises do six to seven of your triceps, etc. (Your triceps are a slightly larger muscle group than your biceps – so you should probably train them a little more.)

This exercise is recommended for body builders and toners. It will also make a nice supplemental lift for athletes and strength trainers.

Kickbacks

Primary muscles targeted and developed: Triceps.

Technique: Stand with your feet shoulder width apart, with knees slightly flexed. Flex at your waist so that your back is almost parallel to the floor. Make sure you keep your back straight (a normal lordosis) with no "humps". Grasp dumbbells in each hand and "lock" your elbows by your side so that your upper arm is also parallel to the floor. Lift the dumbbell by fully extending your arm backwards. Lower the dumbbell (on a 4-second count) until your knuckles point to the floor.

Precautions: Folks with elbow tendonitis or other problems may wish to avoid this lift. If possible use a mirror to confirm proper back alignment.

Spotting: A spotter is not necessary with this lift. You may wish to use one to help with forced reps or negative training.

Notes: You can perform this exercise working both arms at a time or by alternating arms. This exercise recommended for body builders and toners. It will also make a nice supplemental lift for athletes and strength trainers.

Dumbbell "Nose Breakers"

Primary muscles targeted and developed: Triceps.

Technique: Lie on your back (on a supine bench) with your feet flat on the floor. Have a spotter hand you the dumbbells for each hand, above your chest. Hold the dumbbells in a neutral position with your arms extended. Lower the weight toward the sides of your forehead slowly (4 second count). Stop two to three inches above your head and then lift the weight by fully extending your arms. Keep your upper arm stationary, and your elbows pointing up throughout the exercise.

Precautions: Folks with elbow tendonitis or other elbow problems may wish to avoid this lift. This exercise may possibly aggravate shoulder problems. Do not sacrifice technique for weight. Choose a weight that you can manage. This will help you target the triceps and avoid needless injuries (like hitting yourself in the head – there is a logical reason for the name "nose breaker" you know.)

Spotting: A spotter is necessary with this lift. The spotter should assist you by initially handing you the weight as well as being prepared to help during the course of the exercise. The spotter should have his/her hands placed under the dumbbell head throughout the execution of this exercise.

Notes: You can incorporate a combination of nose breaker (until fatigued), then chest press out of this exercise. Recommended for body builders. Athletes and strength trainers may use this exercise as a supplemental lift. Toners and beginners should choose other triceps exercises.

Dumbbell Wrist Curls

Primary muscles targeted and developed: Wrist and Hand flexors.

Technique: Sit on an exercise bench with your forearms resting on your thighs with your palms up (thumbs out). Your knees should be shoulder width apart. If you have not already grasped the dumbbells, have a spotter hand them to you. Lift the weight moving only hands and wrists. Go to full flexion (curl it up as far as you hand will go). Lower the weight on a 3 to 4 second count until your wrist is at full extension.

Precautions: This exercise may possibly aggravate certain elbow and wrist conditions.

Spotting: A spotter is not necessary with this lift. You may wish to use one to help with forced reps.

Notes: This exercise is recommended for athletes, strength trainers, body builders and toners

Reverse Wrist Curls

Primary muscles targeted and developed: Wrist extensors

Technique: Sit on an exercise bench with your forearms resting on your thighs with your palms down (thumbs in). Your knees should be shoulder width apart. If you have not already grasped the dumbbells, have a spotter hand them to you. Lift the weight moving only hands and wrists. Go to full extension (reverse curl it up as far as you hand will go). Lower the weight on a 3 to 4 second count until your wrist is at full flexion.

Precautions: This exercise may possibly aggravate certain elbow and wrist conditions.

Spotting: A spotter is not necessary with this lift. You may wish to use one to help with forced reps.

Notes: This exercise is recommended for athletes, strength trainers, body builders and toners.

CHAPTER 9
Leg Exercises

Well-developed leg muscles will enable you to move about and stand with greater ease. Therefore, if you have a job that requires you to stand quite a bit, stronger legs (developed by resistance training) will make this task easier. The serious cyclist, skater, or sprinter may well have large leg muscles, but they will most likely be lacking in demonstrations of absolute strength. They will also fall short when it comes to their ability to generate power and explosive movement, if they do not supplement their sport with lower body resistance training. Folks who feel they have legs that are too large can reduce this size via an appropriately designed resistance training program.

Step-up

Primary muscles targeted and developed: Quadriceps, Gluteals, and Hamstrings.
Technique: Grasp two dumbbells and hold them by your sides. Position your feet so that they are shoulder width apart. Place your entire foot on the surface of a sturdy box or bench. The platform you use should be 12" to 18" high. While maintaining an erect body position push with your front leg (leg on the box) lifting your body on top of the box. Do not lean forward and do not push off with your back leg.
Precautions: Like the lunge, this exercise is much more back friendly than a squat. However, folks with lower back and knee problems should probably avoid this lift. This lift requires good balance – for that reason you should gradually increase your workload. Start with very light dumbbells and master the movement before increasing the weight.
Spotting: A spotter is not practical with this lift. For that reason is important to train with a relatively light weight.
Notes: This exercise is recommended for strength trainers, athletes, body builders and toners (it really hits the glutes).

Dumbbell Squats

Primary muscles targeted and developed: Quadriceps, Gluteals, Hamstrings, and Spinal erectors.

Technique: Grasp two dumbbells and hold them by your sides. Position your feet so that they are shoulder width, or slightly wider apart. Point your toes slightly out. To lower the weight keep your head up (it may help to focus on a spot close to the ceiling) and your back straight. The dumbbells should remain by your sides throughout the lift. Bend at your knees and hips and slowly (4-5 second count) lower the weight until the tops of your thighs are parallel with the floor. Keep your heels flat on the floor throughout the lift. Do not let your knees travel out past your toes, and keep them aligned with your feet. To lift the weight, maintain the same correct body position. Push from the mid part and heels of your feet. Keep your head back and slowly straighten your knees and hips.

Precautions: People with lower back and knee problems should probably avoid this lift. People with longer extremities may wish to avoid this lift or modify it (quarter squats, sumo squats, etc.)

Spotting: A spotter is not necessary for this lift as it is generally performed with relatively low weight.

Notes: This is a very good alternative to the squat. We recommend this for beginners and folks with shoulder problems. It is also a good exercise for strength trainers, athletes, body builders and toners.

Lunge

Primary muscles targeted and developed: Quadriceps, Gluteals, and Hamstrings.

Technique: Grasp two dumbbells and hold them by your sides. Position your feet shoulder width apart. Take an exaggerated step forward. Bend the knee of your front leg and lower your body until the thigh of this leg is parallel to the floor. Keep your back upright and vertical to the floor. Bend the back knee so that it almost touching the floor when you are at your lowest point. To move back to your original position forcefully push off the floor with your front foot. Bring it back until it is beside your opposite foot. Repeat the same action with the opposite leg.

Precautions: This exercise is much more back friendly than a squat. However, people with low back and knee problems should probably avoid this lift.

Spotting: A spotter should be situated directly behind the lifter - or there should be two spotters, one on each side. Single spotters should move in unison with the lifter and in a similar pattern. This will help keep them in position to help if needed.

Notes: This exercise is recommend for strength trainers, body builders and toners (it really hits the glutes). The lunge and its many variations (back lunge, side lunge, modified lunge and walking lunge) are ideal for the athlete.

Bulgarian Squats

Primary muscles targeted and developed: Glutes, Quadriceps, and Hamstrings.

Technique: Place back foot (toe) on a sturdy platform, box or bench 6" to 18" high. Your other foot should be 1 giant step in front. Hold dumbbells in both hands. The movement and setup of this exercise is like that of a lunge except your rear foot is elevated. Slowly (4 second count) lower your body by bending at the knee of your front leg. The other leg should remain slightly bent throughout this exercise. Lower your body until your lead leg is at a 90-degree angle – When lowering your body do not allow your knee to travel past your toes. This will require you to "sit back" while slightly flexing at the waist. When first attempting this exercise do not use any dumbbells. It may also be necessary to use a support to balance yourself . It is important to master this exercise without the assistance of a support. When you have the movement "down pat" then you should increase the resistance (from just body weight) by holding a dumbbell in both hands.

Precautions: People with possible knee problems should avoid this exercise.

Spotting: When first learning this exercise a spotter is necessary.

Notes: This is one of those exercises that is significantly tougher to perform than you may initially think. This is because proprioception and body control are major factors. The balance and control aspects of this lift, along with the fact that it really hits the glutes and quadriceps are what make it so appealing. Recommended for athletes, strength trainers, body builders and toners.

Standing Heel Raises (Straight Leg Calf Raise)

Primary muscles targeted and developed: Gastrocnemius, Soleus.

Technique: Grasp a dumbbell in each hand and hold in a neutral position. Situate your feet so that the front half (balls of your feet) of your feet are on the platform. Lock your legs so that they are almost fully extended. Allow your heels to drop so that you feel a good stretch in your calf. Lift the weight by pressing down with your feet. Go as high up on your "toes" as possible. At the top of the lift make a conscious effort to squeeze the muscles of your calf and hold the contraction for a minimum of 2 seconds. Lower the weight on a 3 to 4 second count. Repeat the procedure.

Precautions: Ankle and foot injuries as well as Achilles tendonitis can prevent you from safely performing this exercise.

Spotting: A spotter may be necessary to help you maintain balance.

Notes: This exercise is recommended for body builders, toners, strength trainers and athletes.

Sumo Squats

Primary muscles targeted and developed: Quadriceps, Glutes, Leg adductors (inner thigh), and Hamstrings.

Technique: Stand with your feet pointed out, knees slightly bent and your legs spread significantly greater than a shoulder width apart. Hold the head of a dumbbell, with both hands, between your legs (the dumbbell will be vertical to the floor). Keep your back straight. Squat down until the dumbbell head touches the floor, and return to staring position. At this point step to your right – leading with your right foot and sliding your left foot over until you are in your initial stance. Squat until the dumbbell head touches the floor. Repeat this same action to your left.

Precautions: This exercise is significantly more back friendly than a regular squat. However, folks with back problems may wish to avoid this lift. People with knee injuries or problems may need to avoid this lift also.

Spotting: A spotter is not necessary when you perform this exercise.

Notes: This exercise is a natural for athletes as it complements the lateral movement which is associated with most sports. It also targets the inner thigh, which should appeal to many toners. This exercise is recommended for athletes, toners, body builders, and strength trainers.

You can also perform this exercise with a stability ball between your back and a stable wall.

Sumo Squats with Slide

Primary muscles targeted and developed: Quadriceps, Glutes, Leg adductors (inner thigh), and Hamstrings.

Technique: Stand with your feet pointed out, knees slightly bent and your legs spread significantly greater than a shoulder width apart. Hold the head of a dumbbell, with both hands, between your legs (the dumbbell will be vertical to the floor). Keep your back straight. Squat down until the dumbbell head touches the floor, and return to starting position. At this point step to your right – leading with your right foot and sliding your left foot over until you are in your initial stance. Squat until the dumbbell head touches the floor. Repeat this same action to your left.

Precautions: This exercise is significantly more back friendly than a regular squat. However, people with back problems may wish to avoid this lift. People with knee injuries or problems may need to avoid this lift also.

Spotting: A spotter is not necessary when you perform this exercise with a dumbbell. A spotter is needed when this exercise is done with a barbell. The spotter(s) should follow the guidelines for spotting a squat.

Notes: This exercise can be executed with a barbell. It is more difficult to balance yourself with the barbell (and requires spotters), but you are able to train with a larger load (more weight) as opposed to training with the dumbbell. This exercise is a natural for athletes as it complements the lateral movement which is associated with most sports. It also targets the inner thigh, which should appeal to many toners. This exercise is recommended for athletes, toners, body builders, and strength trainers.

You can also perform this exercise with a stability ball between your back and a stable wall (without the slide), or free standing without the slide.

Donkey Raise

Primary muscles targeted and developed: Glutes, Spinal erectors, Hamstrings.

Technique: Situate yourself on "all fours" on the floor. Your hands should be shoulder width apart, and your elbows locked. Your knees should also be shoulder width apart and located directly below your hips, and your head should be slightly lifted. Place a light dumbbell behind your knee (between hamstring and calve), so that the heads are on either side of your leg. Make sure the dumbbell is balanced, and held in place by lifting your foot (flexing your knee). While maintaining good balance, lift your knee until your thigh is parallel with the floor. This should be done on a three to four second count. Lower your knee slowly (three to four seconds) until it almost touches the floor. Repeat this action until the set is complete.

Precautions: People with back problems may wish to avoid this lift.

Spotting: A spotter is not necessary when you perform this exercise.

Notes: It is suggested that you perform this lift on a mat or padded surface for knee comfort. This is an ideal exercise for toners, as it is excellent for sculpting the glutes. It is also recommended for bodybuilders.

Romanian Dead Lifts

Primary muscles targeted and developed: Glutes, Hamstrings, Spinal erectors.

Technique: Stand with feet together and knees slightly bent. Grasp dumbbells in both hands. Allow your arms to hang so that the dumbbells are touching the sides of your thighs. Squeeze your shoulder blades back, and tilt your head back. Slowly (4 second count) lean forward until you feel a good stretch in your hamstrings. The dumbbells should travel beside your legs, and not "drift" away from your body. Make sure to keep your back straight, knees bent and shoulders back throughout the lift. Do not allow your back to become rounded while performing this lift. Return to an upright position on a four-second count. Repeat the process.

Precautions: People with low back problems should avoid this lift.

Spotting: A spotter is not necessary with this lift.

Notes: This is a super glute and hamstring exercise.
Recommended for athletes, body builders, toners (light resistance) and strength trainers.

CHAPTER 10

Olympic Style and Compound Exercises

As was discussed in chapter 4, Olympic style lifting consists of lifts based on the snatch, and clean and jerk – the Olympic lifts preformed in competition. Compound exercises, on the other hand, consist of multiple movements within one set. Both approaches are demanding in nature and require the use of multiple muscle groups to complete the exercise. Compound exercises, for example, may be as simple as executing a dumbbell curl into an Arnold, or as complex as tying a series of lifts in together without any rest. For example, a lunge, to pushup and rotate, to single leg RDL, to single leg row, to a curl into an Arnold and finishing with a triceps extension. Compound exercises are typically designed to include minimal rest periods between movements. This is more conducive to elevating your heart rate, and to a good caloric burn.

Dumbbell Push Press

Primary muscles targeted and developed: Glutes, Quads, Deltoids, and Triceps.

Technique: Stand with feet slightly greater than shoulder width apart, and your toes slightly pointed out. "Rack" the dumbbells at shoulder level (as if performing a shoulder press). Bend (flex) your knees and hips suddenly while maintaining good posture. Rapidly extend your knees and hips with an explosive push from your legs and trunk, while simultaneously extending your arms so that the dumbbells are now above your head. Allow the generated momentum to assist you in lifting the weights. Lower the dumbbells in a controlled, yet somewhat rapid fashion absorbing the weight with your knees. Repeat this sequence until the set is complete

Precautions: People with lower back and shoulder problems should avoid this lift.

Spotting: A spotter is necessary with all beginners and when handling heavy weights.

Notes: This is a very technical lift and requires a great deal of practice with light loads, and the supervision of a knowledgeable fitness professional. Recommended for athletes and strength trainers.

Dumbbell Hang Cleans

Primary muscles targeted and developed: Glutes, Quads, Spinal erectors, Deltoids, and Biceps.

Technique: Stand with feet slightly greater than shoulder width apart, and toes pointed slightly out. Grasp the dumbbells and hold them with your palms facing in slightly above your knees. Bend (flex) your knees and hips suddenly while maintaining good posture. Rapidly extend your knees and hips with an

explosive push from your legs and trunk, while simultaneously pulling the weights up (upright row fashion) to your shoulders. Once the dumbbells reach the shoulder level suddenly "drop" below the weights and catch them at collarbone level. This is the technique you should use to "rack" the weights for performing a push press. Allow the generated momentum to assist you in lifting the weights. Lower the dumbbells in a controlled, yet somewhat rapid fashion absorbing the weight with your knees and hips. Repeat this sequence until the set is complete

Precautions: People with lower back and shoulder problems should avoid this lift.

Spotting: A spotter is necessary with all beginners, and when handling heavy weights.

Notes: This is a very technical lift and requires a great deal of practice with light loads, and the supervision of a knowledgeable fitness professional. Recommended for athletes and strength trainers.

One Arm Dumbbell Snatch

Primary muscles targeted and developed: Glutes, Quads, Spinal erectors, Deltoids, and Triceps.

Technique: Stand with your feet greater than shoulder's width apart. Place the hand of your uninvolved hand on your hip. Let the dumbbell "hang" between

your legs with the involved arm fully extended. Bend (flex) your knees while maintaining good posture. Rapidly extend your knees, while simultaneously pulling the dumbbell (in a upright row movement pattern) explosively. The dumbbell should remain in very close proximity to your body. Continue pulling the dumbbell until it is shoulder level, then suddenly rotate your wrist so that your hand moves from on top of the handle to below it. Allow the generated momentum to assist you in lifting the weight to a position above your head until your arm is fully extended. "Catch" the weight at this point by slightly flexing your hips and knees. Lower the dumbbells in a controlled, yet somewhat rapid fashion absorbing the weight with your knees and hips. Repeat this sequence until the set is complete.

Precautions: People with lower back and shoulder problems should avoid this lift.

Spotting: A spotter is necessary with all beginners and when handling heavy weights.

Notes: This is a very technical lift and requires a great deal of practice with light loads, and the supervision of a knowledgeable fitness professional. Recommended for athletes and strength trainers.

Dumbbell Pushup and Rotate

Primary muscles targeted and developed: Pecs, Deltoids, Triceps, Obliques, Lats and Rhomboids

Technique: Grasp dumbbells in each hand and assume a pushup position on the floor. You body should be supported by your hands (while holding dumbbells) and your feet. Start this exercise with your arms extended. Lower you body toward the floor. Try to get your chest as close to the floor as possible with your back straight — maintaining "tight" abs and lower back. Cross your right foot over your left and extend your arms. In one smooth motion lift the dumbbell in your right hand and rotate your body so that the dumbbell is located above your body. Your arms should be in a straight line with your chest. Your body should now be supported by your left hand and left foot. Slowly lower the weight so that you are back in your original position. Repeat the process to the other side crossing left foot over right and lifting the dumbbell in your left hand.

Precautions: People with lower back and shoulder problems should avoid this lift.

Spotting: A spotter is necessary for beginners and folks training with heavy resistance.

Notes: This is an advanced exercise. It should be first attempted without dumbbells and under the supervision of a fitness professional. Recommended for athletes, body builders, individuals interested in improving body control, and strength trainers.

The Gauntlet

The Gauntlet is a collection of exercises performed in a progression without any rest between sets. As you become more comfortable with the following Gauntlet you will be able to design your own.

The Gauntlet should be designed to target all the major muscle groups of the body. It should also be constructed to offer a workout that will elevate your heart rate, as well as challenge your strength (endurance) and body control.

Primary muscles targeted and developed: All major muscle groups.
Technique: Select a set of dumbbells that will allow you to complete all of the prescribed repetitions and each segment of the Gauntlet with good lifting technique. When first attempting this routine your dumbbells should be very light – sub maximal resistance. Refer to the specific descriptions of each exercise before undertaking this routine.
Progression: Airplane Lunge, Pushup and Rotate, Single leg RDL, Single leg Row, Curl into Arnold, and Triceps Extension.
Precautions: People with lower back and shoulder problems should avoid this lift.
Spotting: A spotter is necessary for beginners. Ideally you should be able to do the Gauntlet without the assistance of a spotter.
Notes: This is an advanced exercise. It should be first attempted under the supervision of a fitness professional. Recommended for athletes, body builders, individuals interested in improving body control and strength trainers.

CHAPTER 11
Body Control Training

Body control exercises are designed to help support and compliment your movements in your every day environment, as well as your most physically demanding activities. Another term for body control training is functional fitness. Examples of situations benefiting from body control (functional) training may include tasks such as vacuuming the floor, or sprinting full speed down basketball court, and changing direction without sacrificing your control or rate of travel.

The following body control exercises are truly unique and very effective in producing results. No matter what your level of lifting experience, you will find these lifts quite rewarding.

The concept behind body control training is to increase the difficulty of the task by placing you in an unstable and unfamiliar environment. This can be accomplished by having you perform the exercises on one foot, for example. The use of a stability ball or rocker board also offer an environment that will assist you in improving your body control, and ability to function better in demanding situations.

Keep in mind, however, these exercises are not easy to perform and even harder to master. They should be considered advanced in nature. Yet, they are not so difficult that a healthy person cannot perform them – Be patient and pay attention to detail and you will have them "down pat" in just a few training sessions.

The bottom line is include these lifts in your training regime and you will be impressed with the gains you see in your strength, body control and physique; no matter what your present level of fitness.

Alternating Dumbbell Press (with feet up)

Primary muscles targeted and developed: Pectoralis major, Anterior deltoids, Triceps, and Trunk stabilizers.

Technique: Start with your back flat on the bench and your knees pointing up so that your feet are off the floor. It is important for balance to start this lift with a dumbbell in each hand. The dumbbells should be situated so that head is touching the side of your chest. Raise one dumbbell in a slight arch above your chest. As you lower that dumbbell raise the other one and vice versa. They should be side by side at a point midway between your chest and full arm extension. Move the dumbbells in a slow controlled manner (4 second count).

Precautions: Shoulder injuries and problems may preclude you from performing this exercise. Start with significantly lighter dumbbells than you would use on a regular dumbbell bench press.

Spotting: Your spotter should be prepared to grab your wrists when assisting. You may wish to use two spotters; one on either side. This will allow them to hand you the dumbbells at a safe beginning position as well as assist you in lowering the dumbbells when finished.

Notes: This exercise is ideal for developing your proprioception and kinesthetic awareness – two terms for balance and body control. Strength athletes quite often make nice jumps in strength after using this as a supplemental lift. This is probably due to muscle fiber recruitment.

Single Leg Romanian Dead Lifts

Primary muscles targeted and developed: Glutes, Hamstrings, Spinal erectors.

Technique: Stand on one foot, with the other foot off the floor and slightly behind it. Grasp dumbbells in both hands. Allow your arms to hang so that the dumbbells are touching the sides of your thighs. Squeeze your shoulder blades back, slightly bend the knee of the "down" foot, and tilt your head back. Slowly (4 second count) lean forward until you feel a good stretch in your hamstrings. Make sure to keep your back straight, knee bent and shoulders back throughout the lift. Do not allow your back to become rounded while performing this lift. Return to an upright position on a 4-second count. Repeat the process.

Precautions: People with lower back problems should avoid this lift.

Spotting: A spotter may be necessary with this lift due to the (sometimes) initial difficulty with body balance.

Notes: This is a super glute and hamstring exercise. Recommended for athletes, body builders, individuals interested in improving body control, and strength trainers.

Single Leg Row

Primary muscles targeted and developed: Glutes, Hamstrings, Spinal erectors.

Technique: Stand on one foot, with the other foot off the floor and slightly behind. Grasp dumbbells in both hands. Squeeze your shoulder blades back, slightly bend the knee of the "down" foot, bend at the waist until it is parallel with the floor and tilt your head back. Allow the dumbbells to hang straight down from your shoulders toward the floor. Make sure to keep your back straight, knee bent and shoulders back throughout the lift. Do not allow your back to become rounded while performing this lift. On a three to four second count pull the dumbbells up until they are level (or touching) with your chest. Repeat the process.

Precautions: People with lower back and shoulder problems should avoid this lift.

Spotting: A spotter may be necessary with this lift due to the (sometime) initial difficulty with body balance.

Notes: Recommended for athletes, body builders, individuals interested in improving body control and strength trainers.

Airplane Lunge

Primary muscles targeted and developed: Glutes, Hamstrings, Spinal erectors, Quads, Deltoids and Rhomboids.

Technique: Stand with your feet shoulder width apart. Allow the dumbbells to hang straight down by your sides. Make sure to keep your shoulders back throughout the lift. Do not allow your back to become rounded while performing this lift. Take an exaggerated step forward with your right foot. Reach with both dumbbells until they are even with your right ankle. Bend both knees so that they are each at an approximate ninety-degree angle. Your back knee should be only a few inches away from the floor. At this point, extend your right knee while simultaneously lifting the dumbbells out from your sides until the are parallel with the floor. At the same time, extend your left leg (point your toe) so that it is also parallel with the floor. Hold this position for a two to three second count. Next straighten your hips (so you are now upright) and step through with your left foot. Repeat the process.

Precautions: People with lower back, knee, and shoulder problems should avoid this lift.

Spotting: A spotter may be necessary with this lift due to the (sometime) initial difficulty with body balance.

Notes: Recommended for athletes, body builders, individuals interested in improving body control and strength trainers.

Balance/Rocker Board Curls

Primary muscles targeted and developed: Biceps brachii, Brachialis, (also muscles of the legs and trunk will be developed as they will assist in balance and control during this lift).

Technique: Stand on the board with your feet completely on the surface, at an equal distance from the edges. Flex slightly at the knee to lower your center of gravity – this is critical for balance. Follow the guidelines for performing a dumbbell curl in the arm exercises chapter. The key to this lift is to perform it with good technique while constantly seeking to balance on the board.

Precautions: In addition to the precautions associated with a dumbbell curl, you need to be aware of safety concerns associated with the balance board. Make sure that the board is on a non-slip surface. Carpeted or rubberized areas are ideal. In order to maintain proper lifting technique and balance, it will be necessary to use a lighter weight than you would with a regular dumbbell curl.

Spotting: You should utilize a spotter when first undertaking this exercise. The spotter is there to assist you if you lose your balance while on the rocker board. Once you become comfortable with the rocker board, a spotter will not be necessary.

Notes: It will be very difficult to complete a set totally balanced on the board. As you adapt, however, finding a balance point and holding it for a relatively long time will become easier. *The key is to constantly seek balance.* You will be surprised at how well your body will adapt. This exercise is recommended for athletes, body builders, strength trainers, toners and individuals interested in improving body control.

Balance/Rocker Board Shoulder Flies

Primary muscles targeted and developed: Deltoids, Trapezius (also muscles of the legs and trunk will be developed as they will assist in balance and control during this lift).

Technique: Stand on the balance board with your feet completely on the surface, at an equal distance from the edges. Flex slightly at the knee to lower your center of gravity – this is critical for balance. Follow the guidelines for performing a dumbbell shoulder fly listed in the shoulder exercise chapter. The key to this lift is to perform it with good technique while constantly seeking to balance on the board.

Precautions: In addition to the precautions associated with a dumbbell fly, you need to be aware of safety concerns associated with the rocker board. Make sure that the board is on a non-slip surface. Carpeted or rubberized areas are ideal. In order to maintain proper lifting technique and balance, it will be necessary to use a lighter weight than you would with a regular dumbbell curl.

Spotting: You should utilize a spotter when first undertaking this exercise. The spotter is there to assist you if you fall off the balance/rocker board. Once you become comfortable with the balance board, a spotter will not be necessary.

Notes: The key is to constantly seek balance. You will be surprised at how well your body will adapt. This exercise is recommended for athletes, body builders, strength trainers and toners.

Balance/Rocker Board Arnold

Primary muscles targeted and developed: Deltoids, Trapezius, and Triceps (also muscles of the legs and trunk will be developed as they will assist in balance and control during this lift).

Technique: Stand on the rocker board with your feet completely on the surface, at an equal distance from the edges. Flex slightly at the knee to lower your center of gravity - this is critical for balance. Follow the guidelines for performing an Arnold in the shoulder exercise chapter. The key to this lift is to perform the exercise with good technique while constantly seeking to balance on the board.

Precautions: In addition to the precautions associated with an Arnold listed in the shoulder exercises chapter, you need to be aware of safety concerns associated with the rocker board. Make sure that the board is on a non-slip surface. Carpeted or rubberized areas are ideal. In order to maintain proper lifting technique and balance, it will be necessary to use a lighter weight than you would with a regular dumbbell curl.

Spotting: You should utilize a spotter when first undertaking this exercise. The spotter is there to assist you if you fall off the balance/rocker board. Once you become comfortable with the balance board, a spotter will not be necessary.

Notes: The key is to constantly seek balance. You will be surprised at how well your body will adapt. This exercise is recommended for athletes, body builders, strength trainers and toners.

Balance/Rocker Board Kickback

Primary muscles targeted and developed: Triceps (also muscles of the legs and trunk will be developed as they will assist in balance and control during this lift).

Technique: Stand on the rocker board with your feet completely on the surface, at an equal distance from the edges. Flex slightly at the knee to lower your center of gravity - this is critical for balance. Follow the guidelines for performing a kickback in the arm exercises chapter. The key to this lift is to perform the exercise with good technique while constantly seeking to balance on the board.

Precautions: In addition to the precautions associated with a dumbbell kickback listed in the arm exercises chapter, you need to be aware of safety concerns associated with the rocker board. Make sure that the board is on a non-slip surface. Carpeted or rubberized areas are ideal. In order to maintain proper lifting technique and balance, it will be necessary to use a lighter weight than you would with a regular dumbbell curl.

Spotting: You should utilize a spotter when first undertaking this exercise. The spotter is there to assist you if you fall off the balance/rocker board. Once you become comfortable with the balance board, a spotter will not be necessary.

Notes: The key is to constantly seek balance. You will be surprised at how well your body will adapt. This exercise is recommended for athletes, body builders, strength trainers and toners.

Stability Ball Dumbbell Press

Primary muscles targeted and developed: Pectoralis major, Anterior deltoids, Triceps, and Trunk stabilizers.

Technique: Start with your buttocks on the floor and your back against the stability ball. It is important for balance to start this lift with a dumbbell in each hand. With your feet shoulder width apart, gradually lift your buttocks off the floor. "Roll" back on the ball until your back is almost parallel to the floor. The dumbbells should be situated so that the head of the dumbbell is touching the side of your chest. Raise the dumbbells in a slight arch (not as great an arch as in the barbell bench) and lightly touch the dumbbell heads once your arms are fully extended. Lower the dumbbells in a very slow controlled manner (4 second count) and repeat.

Precautions: Shoulder conditions may preclude you from performing this exercise. Start with significantly lighter dumbbells than you would use on a regular dumbbell bench press.

Spotting: Your spotter should be prepared to grab your wrists, or stabilize the ball when assisting. You may wish to use two spotters; one on either side. This will allow them to hand you the dumbbells at a safe beginning position as well as assist you in lowering the dumbbells when finished.

Notes: Lower your hips so that your back is at a forty five-degree angle to the floor in order to perform stability ball incline presses. This exercise is ideal for developing your proprioception and kinesthetic awareness – balance and body control. Strength athletes can make nice jumps in strength after using this as a supplemental lift. This is probably due to muscle fiber recruitment. Due to the nature of this exercise it is ideal for developing muscle hypertrophy. You can make this a more taxing exercise by moving your feet closer together. This exercise is recommended for strength trainers, body builders, toners, athletes, and individuals interested in improving body control.

Stability Ball Alternating Dumbbell Press

Primary muscles targeted and developed: Pectoralis major, Anterior deltoids, Triceps, and Trunk stabilizers.

Technique: Start with your buttocks on the floor and your back against the stability ball. It is important for balance to start this lift with a dumbbell in each hand. With your feet shoulder width apart gradually lift your buttocks off the floor. "Roll" back on the ball until your back is almost parallel to the floor. The dumbbells should be situated so that the head of the dumbbell is touching the side of your chest. Raise one dumbbell until your arm is fully extended, and the inside head of the weight is located over the mid-point of the chest. Lower the dumbbell in a very slow controlled manner (4 second count) and raise the opposite one at the same time.

Precautions: Shoulder conditions may preclude you from performing this exercise. Start with significantly lighter dumbbells than you would use on a regular dumbbell bench press.

Spotting: Your spotter should be prepared to grab your wrists, or stabilize the ball when assisting. You may wish to use two spotters; one on either side. This will allow them to hand you the dumbbells at a safe beginning position as well as assist you in lowering the dumbbells when finished.

Notes: Lower your hips so that your back is at a forty five-degree angle to the floor in order to perform stability ball alternating incline presses. This is an advanced exercise and ideal for developing your proprioception and kinesthetic awareness - balance and body control. Strength athletes can make nice jumps in strength after using this as a supplemental lift. This is probably due to muscle fiber recruitment. Due to the nature of this exercise it is ideal for developing muscle hypertrophy. You can make this a more taxing exercise by moving your feet closer together. The alternating dumbbell press is recommended for strength trainers, body builders, toners, athletes and individuals interested in improving body control.

Stability Ball Dumbbell Pullover

Primary muscles targeted and developed: Latisimus dorsi, Pectoralis major, Anterior deltoids, Triceps, and Trunk stabilizers.

Technique: Start with your buttocks on the floor and your back against the stability ball. It is important for balance to start this lift with a dumbbell in each hand and resting on your knees. With your feet a shoulder's width apart gradually lift your buttocks off the floor. "Roll" back on the ball until your back is at a almost parallel to the floor. The dumbbells should be grasped in a neutral position, and lifted so that they are above your chest with your elbows slightly bent. Lower the dumbbells behind your head while keeping your

elbows locked in the same flexed position (4-second count). Allow the dumbbells to go as deep as you can comfortably handle them. You should feel a good stretch in your lats and pecs. Raise the dumbbells in the same arc to the starting position and repeat the process.

Precautions: Shoulder conditions may preclude you from performing this exercise. Start with significantly lighter dumbbells than you would use on a regular dumbbell bench press.

Spotting: Your spotter should be prepared to grab your wrists, or stabilize the ball when assisting. You may wish to use two spotters; one on either side. This will allow them to hand you the dumbbells at a safe beginning position as well as assist you in lowering the dumbbells when finished.

Notes: Lower your hips so that your back is at a forty five-degree angle to the floor in order to perform stability ball incline presses. This exercise is ideal for developing your proprioception and kinesthetic awareness – balance and body control. Strength athletes can make nice jumps in strength after using this as a supplemental lift. This is probably due to muscle fiber recruitment. Due to the nature of this exercise it is ideal for developing muscle hypertrophy. You can make this a more taxing exercise by moving your feet closer together. This exercise is recommended for strength trainers, body builders, toners, athletes, and individuals interested in improving body control.

Stability Ball Arnold's

Primary muscles targeted and developed: Deltoids, Trapezius, and Triceps, Trunk stabilizers.

Technique: Initiate this exercise by sitting upright on the stability ball. Keep your body erect with good posture. The starting position and the initial upward movement of this exercise are what distinguish it from a regular dumbbell shoulder press. You should grasp the dumbbells firmly and hold them at chest level with your palms facing in. Lift the weight and turn your palms out simultaneously until your arms are fully extended. At the peak of the lift your palms should be facing out. The dumbbell heads should be touching at the start of each rep and again (the opposite heads this time) at the end of each rep. Movements should be controlled, and the weights lowered on a four-second count.

Precautions: Due to the unstable environment in which this exercise is performed, even greater than normal shoulder and back (posture) precautions should be taken. When first initiating this exercise use very light resistance.

Spotting: It is necessary to have a spotter throughout the execution of this exercise. The spotter should be prepared to grab the lifter's wrist (as opposed to the elbows) or stabilize the ball if help is needed.

Notes: This exercise will incorporate help from the muscles supporting the trunk, the pecs, and supporting muscles around the shoulder. This exercise is recommended for athletes, strength trainers, body builders, and toners.

Stability Ball Dumbbell Curls

Primary muscles targeted and developed: Biceps brachii, Brachialis, Brachioradialis and Trunk stabilizing muscles.

Technique: Sit on the stability ball with your back straight (good posture) and your feet flat on the floor shoulder width apart. Grasp the dumbbells firmly in each hand and extend your arms. The dumbbells should be slightly below your hips lightly touching the surface of the ball. Bring the dumbbells up by bending (flexing) your arms at the elbow. Rotate your hands so that at the bottom of the lift you have a neutral grip and at the top your palms are facing in. Your elbows should remain locked at your side. Raise the dumbbells until they are just a few inches away from your deltoids. Do not let the dumbbells "rest" at the height of the lift. Lower the dumbbells on a four-second count until arms are fully extended.

Precautions: Persons with elbow and shoulder problems may choose to avoid this exercise.

Spotting: When first learning this exercise a spotter is necessary to help stabilize the ball.

Notes: Increase the demands of this exercise by moving your feet closer together. Recommended for athletes, strength trainers, body builders, individuals interested in improving body control, and toners.

Stability Ball Shoulder Flies

Primary muscles targeted and developed: Deltoids, Trapezius, and, Trunk stabilizers.

Technique: Initiate this exercise by sitting upright on the stability ball. Keep your body erect with good posture. The starting position and the initial upward movement of this exercise are what distinguish it from a regular dumbbell shoulder press. You should grasp the dumbbells firmly and hold them at chest level with your palms facing in. Lift the weight and turn your palms out simultaneously until your arms are fully extended. At the peak of the lift your palms should be facing out. The dumbbell heads should be touching at the start of each rep and again (the opposite heads this time) at the end of each rep. Movements should be controlled, and the weights lowered on a four-second count.

Precautions: Due to the unstable environment in which this exercise is performed, even greater than normal shoulder and back posture precautions should be taken. When first initiating this exercise use very light resistance.

Spotting: It is necessary to have a spotter throughout the execution of this exercise. The spotter should be prepared to grab the lifter's wrist (as opposed to the elbows) if help is needed.

Notes: This exercise will incorporate help from the muscles supporting the trunk, the pecs, and supporting muscles around the shoulder. This exercise is recommended for athletes, strength trainers, body builders, and toners.

Stability Ball Bulgarian Squats

Primary muscles targeted and developed: Glutes, Quadriceps, and Hamstrings.

Technique: Place back foot (toe) on a stability ball. Have a spotter hold the ball initially in order to help you gain body control. Your other foot should be 1 giant step in front. Hold the dumbbells in both hands. The movement and setup of this exercise is like that of a lunge except your rear foot is elevated. Slowly (4 second count) lower your body by bending at the knee of your front leg. The other leg should remain slightly bent throughout this exercise. Lower your body until your lead leg is at a ninety-degree angle. While lowering your body do not allow your knee to travel past your toes. This will require you to "sit back" while slightly flexing at the waist. When first attempting this exercise, do not use any dumbbells. It is important to master this exercise without the assistance of a support. When you have mastered the movement, then you should increase the resistance (from just body weight) by holding a dumbbell in each hand.

Precautions: Persons with knee problems should avoid this exercise.

Spotting: When first learning this exercise a spotter is necessary.

Notes: This is one of those exercises that are significantly tougher to perform than you may initially think. This is because proprioception and body control are major factors. The balance and control aspects of this lift, along with the fact that it really hits the glutes and quadriceps are what make it so appealing. Recommended for athletes, strength trainers, body builders, individuals interested in improving body control, and toners.

Stork Exercises

Stork exercises are ideal for developing body control and balance. They are also quite simple to incorporate. Each exercise is initiated the same way. Stand on one foot, lift the other foot off the ground, and place it on the calf of your weight bearing leg. Slightly flex (bend) the knee of your supporting leg and prepare to perform virtually any exercise you can perform standing on both feet. For example: dumbbell curls, Arnold's, shoulder flies, triceps extensions, bentover flies, kickbacks, and bent over rows.

The keys to executing stork exercises are quite simple. Train on each leg equally and keep good posture throughout each lift. Keep your knee slightly flexed and your foot flat on the floor throughout each exercise. To maintain balance, focus on a spot ahead you and concentrate on executing the lift with proper technique.

Incorporate stork exercises (or other body control exercises) in the middle of your regular lifting session, or dedicate entire lifting sessions to this type of routine. The variety offered from this type of approach is refreshing, and the results you will experience will be quite rewarding.

CHAPTER **12**

Sample Routines

Use this chapter, and the sample routines it includes, as a model for designing your own program. For specific help regarding program design, refer back to chapters 3 and 4. Keep in mind that there are no absolute steps to developing your body. Your body may not respond exactly like your partners to the same routine. So you should be somewhat flexible in your approach, and willing to change your routine on occasion.

It is very important for you to know that the information we share with you in this book is very sound and effective if applied in a safe and appropriate manner. Therefore, we will guarantee that no matter what your level of fitness, if you follow the principles and guidelines we present, remain healthy, and incorporate the exercises we share you will make very significant and positive gains in your fitness and physique.

Beginner Program (Regardless of Goals)

When you are starting a resistance training program it is very important that you allow your body (particularly your muscles) an acclimation period. In other words, your body deserves, and needs, a good introduction to this new stimulus it is about to encounter. This is important no matter what your ultimate goal: strength gains, increases in muscle size, better body tone or improved athletic performance. The following beginner routine is designed to allow for optimal adaptation to training.

Please remember that this routine, as well as the ones to follow, is not written in stone. Make changes where necessary; just make sure you follow the principles and guidelines laid out for you in this book.

Week 1 & 2 (Circuit Training)

2 Days (i.e. Monday and Friday)			
Exercise	Repetitions	Load	Rest Period
Chest Press	12-14	50-75% of Max	1 Min.
Dumbbell Rows	12-14	50-75% of Max	1 Min.
Shoulder Press	12-14	50-75% of Max	1 Min.
Dumbbell Curls	12-14	50-75% of Max	1 Min.
Triceps Kickbacks	12-14	50-75% of Max	1 Min.
Lunges	12-14	50-75% of Max	1 Min.
Rumanian Dead Lifts (RDL)	12-14	50-75% of Max	1 Min.
Heel Raises	20-24	50-75% of Max	1 Min.

Week 3

2 Days (i.e. Monday and Friday)				
Exercise	Sets	Repetitions	Load (Set1/Set2)	Rest Period
Chest Press	2	10-12	50%/75%	1 Min.
Pull Overs	2	10-12	50%/75%	1 Min.
Lateral Flies	2	10-12	50%/75%	1 Min.
Dumbbell Curls	2	10-12	50%/75%	1 Min.
Triceps Extensions	2	10-12	50%/75%	1 Min.
Sumo Squats	2	10-12	50%/75%	1 Min.
Lunge Walk	2	10-12	50%/75%	1 Min.
Heel Raises	2	20-24	50%/75%	1 Min.

Week 4

2 Days (i.e. Monday and Friday)				
Exercise	Sets	Repetitions	Load (Set1/Set2)	Rest Period
Chest Press	2	10-12	50%/100%	1 Min.
Dumbbell Row	2	10-12	50%/100%	1 Min.
Lateral Flies	2	10-12	50%/100%	1 Min.
Dumbbell Curls	2	10-12	50%/100%	1 Min.
Triceps Kickbacks	2	10-12	50%/100%	1 Min.
Lunges	2	10-12	50%/100%	1 Min.
RDL	2	10-12	50%/100%	1 Min.
Heel Raises	2	20-24	50%/100%	1 Min.

NOTE: This routine is designed to introduce you to a variety of resistance exercises, and to allow for optimal adaptation. The percentages under the load category are based on your repetition maximum (RM) (i.e. 50% of a 12 to 14 repetition maximum). Initially this will require some guesswork on your part. By week three however, with a partner's assistance, you should be able to reasonably establish your estimated multiple repetition maximums with each exercise.

Strength Training Routine
(4 Days a Week i.e. Mon., Tues., Thurs., Fri.)

Weeks 1-4

Day 1		
Core Lifts	**Percentage of 1 RM and Reps**	**Rest Period**
Chest Press	60%x10, 70%x8, 75%x8, 80%x8, 85%x6	1.5 Min.
Dumbbell Rows	60%x10, 70%x8, 75%x8, 80%x8, 85%x6	1.5 Min.
Shoulder Press	60%x10, 75%x8, 85%x6	1.5 Min.
Aux. Lifts	**Sets and Reps**	**Rest Period**
Dumbbell Flies	3 x 7-9 RM	1.5 Min.
Pull Overs	3 x 7-9 RM	1.5 Min.
Dumbbell Curls	3 x 7-9 RM	1.5 Min.
Triceps Extensions	3 x 7-9 RM	1.5 Min.

Day 2		
Core Lifts	**Percentage of 1 RM and Reps**	**Rest Period**
Squat	60%x10, 70%x8, 75%x8, 80%x8, 85%x6	1.5 Min.
Dead Lift	60%x10, 70%x8, 75%x8, 80%x8, 85%x6	1.5 Min.
Lunges	60%x10, 75%x8, 85%x6	1.5 Min.
Aux. Lifts	**Sets and Reps**	**Rest Period**
Single Leg RDL	3 x 7-9 RM	1.5 Min.
Bulgarian Squat	3 x 7-9 RM	1.5 Min. Heel
Raises	3 x 7-9 RM	1.5 Min.

Day 3		
Core Lifts	Percentage of 1 RM and Reps	Rest Period
Chest Press	60%x10, 70%x8, 75%x8, 80%x8, 85%x6	1.5 Min.
Dumbbell Rows	60%x10, 70%x8, 75%x8, 80%x8, 85%x6	1.5 Min.
Shoulder Press	60%x10, 70%x8, 85%x6	1.5 Min.
Aux. Lifts	Sets and Reps	Rest Period
Incline Dumbbell Press	3 x 7-9 RM	1.5 Min.
Pull Overs	3 x 7-9 RM	1.5 Min.
Hammer Curls	3 x 7-9 RM	1.5 Min.
Nose Breakers	3 x 7-9 RM	1.5 Min

Day 4		
Core Lifts	Percentage of 1 RM and Reps	Rest Period
Squat	60%x10, 70%x8, 75%x8, 80%x8, 85%x6	1.5 Min.
RDL	60%x10, 70%x8, 75%x8, 80%x8, 85%x6	1.5 Min.
Lunges	60%x10, 75%x8, 85%x6	1.5 Min.
Aux. Lifts	Sets and Reps	Rest Period
Single Leg RDL	3 x 7-9 RM	1.5 Min.
Step Ups	3 x 7-9 RM	1.5 Min.
Heel Raises	3 x 7-9 RM	1.5 Min.

Weeks 5-8

Day 1		
Core Lifts	Percentage of 1 RM and Reps	Rest Period
Chest Press	60%x10, 75%x6, 80%x4 85%x4, 90%x4	2 Min.
Dumbbell Rows	60%x10, 75%x6, 80%x4 85%x4, 90%x4	2 Min.
Shoulder Press	60%x10, 85%x4, 90%x4	2 Min.
Aux. Lifts	Sets and Reps	Rest Period
Dumbbell Incline Press	3 x 4-6 RM	2 Min.
Pull Overs	3 x 4-6 RM	2 Min.
Dumbbell Curls	3 x 4-6 RM	2 Min.
Triceps Extensions	3 x 4-6RM	2 Min.

Day 2		
Core Lifts	**Percentage of 1 RM and Reps**	**Rest Period**
Squat	60%x10, 75%x6, 80%x4 85%x4, 90%x4	2 Min.
RDL	60%x10, 75%x6, 80%x4 85%x4, 90%x4	2 Min.
Lunges	60%x10, 85%x4, 90%x4	2 Min.
Aux. Lifts	**Sets and Reps**	**Rest Period**
Single Leg RDL	3 x 4-6 RM	2 Min.
Step-ups	3 x 4-6 RM	2 Min.
Heel Raises	3 x 4-6 RM	2 Min.

Day 3		
Core Lifts	**Percentage of 1 RM and Reps**	**Rest Period**
Chest Press	60%x10,75%x6, 80%x4 85%x4, 90%x4	2 Min.
Dumbbell Row	60%x10,75%x6, 80%x4 85%x4, 90%x4	2 Min.
Shoulder Press	60%x10, 85%x4, 90%x4	2 Min.
Aux. Lifts	**Sets and Reps**	**Rest Period**
Dumbbell Incline Press	3 x 4-6 RM	2 Min.
Pull Overs	3 x 4-6 RM	2 Min.
Hammer Curls	3 x 4-6 RM	2 Min.
Nose Breakers	3 x 4-6 RM	2 Min.

Day 4		
Core Lifts	**Percentage of 1 RM and Reps**	**Rest Period**
Squat	60%x10,75%x6, 80%x4 85%x4, 90%x4	2 Min.
RDL	60%x10,75%x6, 80%x4 85%x4, 90%x4	2 Min.
Lunges	60%x10, 85%x4, 90%x4	2 Min.
Aux. Lifts	**Sets and Reps**	**Rest Period**
Single Leg RDL	3 x 4-6 RM	2 Min.
Step Ups	3 x 4-6 RM	2 Min.
Heel Raises	3 x 4-6 RM	2 Min.

Week 9-10

Day 1		
Core Lifts	**Percentage of 1 RM and Reps**	**Rest Period**
Chest Press	60%x10, 75%x5, 85%x5, 95%x2, 105%x1	2.5 Min.
Dumbbell Rows	60%x10, 75%x5, 85%x5, 95%x2, 105%x1	2.5 Min.
Shoulder Press	60%x10, 85%x4, 90%x4	2.5 Min.
Aux. Lifts	**Sets and Reps**	**Rest Period**
Dumbbell Incline Press	3 x 2-3 RM	2.5 Min.
Pull Overs	3 x 2-3 RM	2.5 Min.
Dumbbell Curls	3 x 4-6 RM	2.5 Min.
Triceps Extensions	3 x 4-6 RM	2.5 Min..

Day 2		
Core Lifts	**Percentage of 1 RM and Reps**	**Rest Period**
Squat	60%x10, 75%x5, 85%x5, 95%x2, 105%x1	2.5 Min.
RDL	60%x10, 75%x5, 85%x5, 95%x2	2.5 Min.
Lunges	60%x10, 85%x4, 90%x4	2.5 Min.
Aux. Lifts	**Sets and Reps**	**Rest Period**
Single Leg RDL	3 x 4-6 RM	2.5 Min.
Step Ups	3 x 4-6 RM	2.5 Min.
Heel Raises	3 x 4-6 RM	2.5 Min.

Day 3		
Core Lifts	**Percentage of 1 RM and Reps**	**Rest Period**
Chest Press	60%x10, 75%x5, 85%x5, 95%x2, 105%x1	2.5 Min.
Dumbbell Rows	60%x10, 75%x5, 85%x5, 95%x2, 105%x1	2.5 Min.
Shoulder Press	60%x10, 85%x4, 90%x4	2.5 Min.
Aux. Lifts	**Sets and Reps**	**Rest Period**
Dumbbell Incline Press	3 x 2-3 RM	2.5 Min.
Pull Overs	3 x 2-3 RM	2.5 Min.
Hammer Curls	3 x 4-6 RM	2.5 Min.
Nose Breakers	3 x 4-6 RM	2.5 Min.

Day 4		
Core Lifts	**Percentage of 1 RM and Reps**	**Rest Period**
Squat	60%x10, 75%x5, 85%x5, 95%x2, 105%x1	2.5 Min.
RDL	60%x10, 75%x5, 85%x5, 95%x2	2.5 Min.
Lunges	60%x10, 85%x4, 90%x4	2.5 Min.
Aux. Lifts	**Sets and Reps**	**Rest Period**
Single Leg RDL	3 x 4-6 RM	2.5 Min.
Step Ups	3 x 4-6 RM	2.5 Min.
Heel Raises	3 x 4-6 RM	2.5 Min.

Week 11

Active rest, No strength training.

NOTE: This is truly an advanced program and should only be used by serious strength trainers. It will be necessary to obtain your one-rep maximums on all your core lifts. It will also be necessary to use a little math to compute the amount of weight to use with each lift. (There are software programs available that will do this for you, as well as assist you in the design of your program.) The week (11) of active rest is very important as it is designed to allow for recovery before starting the program over again at week one.

It is important that you complete every repetition of the last set of each exercise. Have your spotter assist you with forced reps when necessary. Also "listen" to your body. In other words, avoid overtraining by eliminating or abbreviating the auxiliary lifts on days that your muscles feel especially fatigued.

The Romanian Dead Lifts (RDL) are designed to target the glutes and hamstrings primarily. There is an obvious risk of injury to the lower back if this exercise is not performed with correct technique. Use extreme caution when incorporating this lift. Reduce the amount of weight lifted throughout the cycle if you feel uncomfortable handling larger loads.

Please note that abdominal and trunk specific (core) exercises, as well as cardiovascular exercises are not included. These are two very important areas of any training regime and should be incorporated. Utilize the help of a fitness professional for the appropriate approach to abdominal (core) and cardiovascular training.

NOTE: Squats may be substituted with Sumo Squats.

Body Building (Split) Routine (3 days on, 2 days off)

Day 1 (Chest and Triceps)			
Exercise	Sets	Repetitions	Rest Period
Chest Press	3	12-14 RM	1 Min.
Alt Dumbbell Press	3	12-14 RM	1 Min.
Dumbbell (DB) Incline Press	3	12-14 RM	1 Min.
DB Decline Press	3	12-14 RM	1 Min.
Triceps Kickbacks	3	12-14 RM	1 Min.
Triceps Extension	3	12-14 RM	1 Min.
Nose Breakers	3	12-14 RM	1 Min.

Day 2 (Back and Biceps)			
Exercise	Sets	Repetitions	Rest Period
Pull Overs	3	12-14 RM	1 Min.
Dumbbell Rows	3	12-14 RM	1 Min.
Bent over Flies	3	12-14 RM	1 Min.
Shrugs	3	12-14 RM	1 Min.
Dumbbell Curls	3	12-14 RM	1 Min.
Hammer Curls	3	12-14 RM	1 Min.
Concentration Curls	3	12-14 RM	1 Min.

Day 3 (Legs and Shoulders)			
Exercise	Sets	Repetitions	Rest Period
Squats	3	12-14 RM	1 Min.
Lunges	3	12-14 RM	1 Min.
Bulgarian Squats	3	12-14 RM	1 Min.
Single Leg RDL	3	12-14 RM	1 Min.
Heel Raises	3	20-24 RM	1 Min.
Shoulder Press	3	12-14 RM	1 Min.
Arnolds	3	12-14 RM	1 Min.
Upright Row	3	12-14 RM	1 Min.

Days 4 and 5

Active Rest; No Lifting

Day 6 (Chest and Triceps)			
Exercise	Sets	Repetitions	Rest Period
Chest Press	3	12-14 RM	1 Min.
Dumbbell Flies	3	12-14 RM	1 Min.
Incline DB Press	3	12-14 RM	1 Min.
Dumbbell Press Drop Set- Progress through 5 total sets starting with a 12-14 RM.			
Triceps Ext.	3	12-14 RM	1 Min.
Nose Breakers	3	12-14 RM	1 Min.
Triceps Kickbacks Drop Set- Progress through 5 total sets starting with a 12-14 RM.			

Day 7 (Back and Biceps)			
Exercise	Sets	Repetitions	Rest Period
Bentover Flies	3	12-14 RM	1 Min.
Shrugs	3	12-14 RM	1 Min.
Dumbbell Row	3	12-14 RM	1 Min.
Pull Overs Drop Set- Progress through 5 total sets starting with a 12-14 RM.			
Dumbbell Curls	3	12-14 RM	1 Min.
Incline DB Curls	3	12-14 RM	1 Min.
Concentration Curls Drop Set- Progress through 5 total sets starting with a 12-14 RM.			

Day 8 (Legs and Shoulders)			
Exercise	Sets	Repetitions	Rest Period
Squats	3	12-14 RM	1 Min.
Sumo Squats	3	12-14 RM	1 Min.
Romanian D-Lifts	3	12-14 RM	1 Min.
Lunge Drop Set- Progress through 5 total sets starting with a 12-14 RM.			
Single Leg RDL Drop Set- Progress through 5 total sets starting with a 12-14 RM.			
Heel Raises	3	20-24 RM	1 Min.
Shoulder Press	3	12-14 RM	1 Min.
Arnolds	3	12-14 RM	1 Min.
Lateral Flies Drop Set- Progress through 5 total sets starting with a 12-14 RM.			

Days 9 and 10

Active Rest; No Lifting

NOTES: Follow this format for a total of 30 days. At the end of a 30-day cycle, change the rep frame to an 8-10 RM. Your rest periods between sets should be slightly increased to 1.5 minutes. You may choose to replace drop sets with forced rep and negative training occasionally. Substitute lifts periodically as well. Keep in mind that it is extremely important to find a sound balance between variety and consistency. Identify certain body part lifts as core lifts and keep them as staples in your program.

At the end of the second 30-day cycle, incorporate a 10-day cycle of 6-8 RM training. This will help your strength gains as well as being important in your efforts for muscle hypertrophy.

Toning Workout (2 Days a Week i.e. Mon., Thur.)

Day 1			
Exercise	Sets	Repetitions	Rest Period
Chest Press	2	14-16 RM	1 Min.
Pull Overs	2	14-16 RM	1 Min.
Shoulder Press	2	14-16 RM	1 Min.
Dumbbell Curls	2	14-16 RM	1 Min.
Triceps Kickbacks	2	14-16 RM	1 Min.
Lunges	2	14-16 RM	1 Min.
RDL	2	14-16 RM	1 Min.
Step Ups	2	14-16 RM	1 Min.
Heel Raises	2	24-28 RM	1 Min.

Day 2 (Circuit Training)	
Exercise	Reps
Chest Press	14-16 RM
Crunches	10
Pull Overs	14-16 RM
Crunches	10
Shoulder Press	14-16 RM
Crunches	10
Dumbbell Curls	14-16 RM
Crunches	10
Triceps Extensions	14-16 RM
Lunge Walk	20 to 30 Steps

NOTE: Move from station to station in as rapid a fashion as possible, while maintaining good sound technique. At the end of the circuit rest for 3 minutes and then repeat.

Day 3			
Exercise	Sets	Repetitions	Rest Period
Dumbbell Press	2	14-16 RM	1 Min.
Dumbbell Rows	2	14-16 RM	1 Min.
Shoulder Press	2	14-16 RM	1 Min.
Dumbbell Curls	2	14-16 RM	1 Min.
Triceps Kickback	2	14-16 RM	1 Min.
Lunge	2	14-16 RM	1 Min.
Step Ups	2	14-16 RM	1 Min.
RDL	2	14-16RM	1 Min.
Heel Raises	2	24-28RM	1 Min.

NOTES: Continue to rotate routines throughout your training cycle. At the end of a 12-week training period change many of your exercises and add 2 reps to each set. Make a focused effort to increase the weight you are training with on a regular basis. Every time you reach a point where you can complete 17 reps on a exercise that calls for a 14-16 RM, increase your training load.

Athletic Enhancement (Pre-Season and Post Season Routine)

(3 Days a Week, i.e. Mon., Wed., Fri.)

There are certain athletic traits that are essential for success in most sports. Speed, strength, explosive movement, and body control represent areas of athleticism common to the outstanding player. How many truly great soccer, basketball, football, tennis, baseball, or volleyball (the list could go on and on) stars can you name that do not possess a high level of at least one of these traits? Our guess is not many. Could U.S. soccer great, Mia Hamm, score all those goals without super leg power and body control? Do you think Mark McGwire and Sammy Sosa could hit all those home runs without tremendous upper body power? Could John Stockton consistently blow by defenders to score without outstanding explosive movement and body control? The answer to these questions is a resounding NO! At the highest levels of sport the characteristic that routinely separates the star from the average player is not the level of their sport specific skills, but rather the level of their athleticism. If everything else is equal then "you can bet the farm" that the faster, better controlled, or more explosive athlete is going to come out on top.

The first and perhaps most important step to improving athleticism is building a sound strength base. The strength training routine we are sharing is designed for the athlete, but somewhat generic in nature. You are provided with a 3-day a week program with which many athletes have experienced a great deal of success. Many strength and conditioning experts prefer a four-day program that resembles the strength training routine outlined earlier in this chapter. If given the time and opportunity, this book would include routines designed to meet the needs of specific sports. However, the program provided will benefit in all athletes involved sports requiring speed, strength, explosive movement, or body control. This routine represents a pre-season, or post-season, program.

In-season training has not been specifically addressed. An in-season resistance training routine is extremely important and should be designed to meet the demands of your competitive schedule. Your workload in the weight room should be significantly reduced in-season. Avoid resistance training on days of competition. Do not underestimate the importance of in-season strength training. It is essential for consistent play, and for reducing the risk of injury – not to mention it helps you look and feel better.

Weeks 1-4

Day 1		
Core Lifts	**Percentage of 1 RM and Reps**	**Rest Period**
Chest Press	60% x 10, 70% x 8, 75% x 8, 80% x 8	1.5 Min.
Dumbbell Rows	60% x 10, 70% x 8, 75% x 8, 80% x 8	1.5 Min.
Shoulder Press	60% x 10, 75% x 8, 85% x 6	1.5 Min.
Squats	60% x 10, 70% x 8, 75% x 8, 80% x 8	1.5 Min.
RDL	60% x 10, 70% x 8, 75% x 8, 80% x 8	1.5 Min.
Optional Lifts	**Sets and Reps**	**Rest Period**
DB Incline Press	3 x 8-10 RM	1.5 Min.
Pull Overs	3 x 8-10 RM	1.5 Min.
Dumbbell Curls	3 x 8-10 RM	1.5 Min.
Triceps Extensions	3 x 8-10 RM	1.5 Min.

Day 2			
Exercise	**Sets**	**Repetitions**	**Rest Period**
Alt. Dumbbell Press	3	8-10	1 Min.
Pull Overs w/ Crunch	3	8-10	1 Min.
Balance Board Arnolds	3	8-10	1 Min.
Balance Board Curls	3	8-10	1 Min.
Balance Board Kickback	3	8-10	1 Min.
Sumo Squats	4	8-10	1 Min.
Airplane Lunge	4	8-10	1 Min.
Single Leg RDL	3	8-10	1 Min.
Heel Raises	4	8-10	1 Min.

Day 3		
Core Lifts	**Percentage of 1 RM and Reps**	**Rest Period**
DB Incline Press	60% x 10, 70% x 8, 75% x 8, 80% x 8	1.5 Min.
Dumbbell Rows	60% x 10, 70% x 8, 75% x 8, 80% x 8	1.5 Min.
Upright Row	60% x 10, 75% x 8, 85% x 6	1.5 Min.
Squats	60% x 10, 70% x 8, 75% x 8, 80% x 8	1.5 Min.
RDL	60% x 10, 70% x 8, 75% x 8, 80% x 8	1.5 Min.
Optional Lifts	**Sets and Reps**	**Rest Period**
Dumbbell Press	3 x 8-10 RM	1.5 Min.
Pull Overs	3 x 8-10 RM	1.5 Min.
Lunges	3 x 8-10 RM	1.5 Min.
Single RDL	3 x 8-10 RM	1.5 Min.
Heel Raises	3 x 20-24 RM	1.5 Min.

Weeks 5-8

Day 1		
Core Lifts	**Percentage of 1 RM and Reps**	**Rest Period**
Chest Press	60%x10, 75%x6, 85%x4, 95%x4	2 Min.
Dumbbell Row	60%x10, 75%x6, 85%x4, 95%x4	2 Min.
Shoulder Press	60%x10, 85%x6, 95%x4	2 Min.
Squats	60%x10, 75%x6, 85%x4, 95%x4	2 Min.
RDL	60%x10, 75%x6, 85%x4, 95%x4	2 Min.

Optional Lifts	Sets and Reps	Rest Period
DB Incline Press	3 x 6-8 RM	2 Min.
Pull Overs	3 x 6-8 RM	2 Min.
Dumbbell Curls	3 x 6-8 RM	2 Min.
Triceps Extensions	3 x 6-8 RM	2 Min.

Day 2			
Exercise	Sets	Repetitions	Rest Period
Stability Ball Chest Press	3	6-8	2 Min.
Pull Overs	3	6-8	2 Min.
Balance Board Arnolds	3	6-8	2 Min.
Balance Board Curls	3	6-8	2 Min.
Balance Board Kickback	3	6-8	2 Min.
Stability Ball Bulgarians	4	6-8	2 Min.
Single Leg RDL	4	6-8	2 Min.
Air Plane Lunge	3	6-8	2 Min.
Heel Raises	4	20-22	2 Min.

Day 3		
Core Lifts	Percentage of 1 RM and Reps	Rest Period
DB Incline Press	60% x 10, 75% x 6, 85% x 4, 95% x 4	2 Min.
Dumbbell Row	60% x 10, 75% x 6, 85% x 4, 95% x 4	2 Min.
Upright Row	60% x 10, 85% x 6, 95% x 4	2 Min.
Squats	60% x 10, 75% x 6, 85% x 4, 95% x 4	2 Min.
RDL	60% x 10, 75% x 6, 85% x 4, 95% x 4	2 Min.
Optional Lifts	Sets and Reps	Rest Period
Dumbbell Press	3 x 6-8 RM	2 Min.
Pull Overs	3 x 6-8 RM	2 Min.
Lunges	3 x 6-8 RM	2 Min.
Single Leg RDL	3 x 6-8 RM	2 Min.
Heel Raises	3 x 18-22 RM	2 Min.

Weeks 9-10

Day 1		
Core Lifts	**Percentage of 1 RM and Reps**	**Rest Period**
Chest Press	60% x 10, 80% x 5, 90% x 5, 100% x 2	2.5 Min.
Dumbbell Rows	60% x 10, 80% x 5, 90% x 5, 100% x 2	2.5 Min.
Shoulder Press	60% x 10, 95% x 4, 100% x 2	2.5 Min.
Squats	60% x 10, 80% x 5, 90% x 5, 100% x 2	2.5 Min.
RDL	60% x 10, 80% x 5, 90% x 5, 100% x 2	2.5 Min.
Optional Lifts	**Sets and Reps**	**Rest Period**
DB Incline Press	3 x 4-6 RM	2.5 Min.
Pull Overs	3 x 4-6 RM	2.5 Min.
Dumbbell Curls	3 x 4-6 RM	2.5 Min.
Triceps Extensions	3 x 4-6 RM	2.5 Min.

Day 2			
Exercise	**Sets**	**Repetitions**	**Rest Period**
Alt. Dumbbell Press	3	4-6	2.5 Min.
Pull Overs w/Crunch	3	4-6	2.5 Min.
Wobble Board Arnolds	3	4-6	2.5 Min.
Wobble Board Curls	3	6-8	2 Min.
Wobble Board Kickback	3	6-8	2 Min.
Sumo Squats	4	4-6	2.5 Min.
Single Leg RDL	4	4-6	2.5 Min.
Stability Ball Bulgarian Squats	3	4-6	2.5 Min.
Heel Raises	4	16-18	2.5 Min.

Day 3		
Core Lifts	**Percentage of 1 RM and Reps**	**Rest Period**
DB Incline Press	60% x 10, 80% x 5, 90% x 5, 100% x 2	2.5 Min.
Dumbbell Rows	60% x 10, 80% x 5, 90% x 5, 100% x 2	2.5 Min.
Upright Row	60% x 10, 90% x 5,100% x 2	2.5 Min.
Squats	60% x 10, 80% x 5, 90% x 5, 100% x 2	2.5 Min.
RDL	60% x 10, 80% x 5, 90% x 5, 100% x 2	2.5 Min.

Optional Lifts	Sets and Reps	Rest Period
Dumbbell Press	3 x 4-6 RM	2.5 Min.
Pull Overs	3 x 4-6 RM	2.5 Min.
Lunges	3 x 6-8 RM	2.5 Min.
Single Leg RDL	3 x 20/10/10/20	2.5 Min.
Heel Raises	3 x 18-22 RM	2.5 Min.

Week 11

This is a period of active rest – no resistance training.

NOTES: Resistance training is a very important part of developing total athleticism. However, an athlete should never assume that resistance training is enough in and of itself to provide total performance enhancement. It is just one cog (a major one grant you) in a very elaborate machine. This routine should be accompanied by sport specific conditioning, abdominal and core training, stretching, as well as speed, quickness, body control, and power development drills.

Once you have completed an 11-week cycle, start over again. Each subsequent training cycle will most likely be performed at a higher level than the last.

Body Control Training (3 days a week, i.e. Mon, Wed, Thur)

Body control training is a somewhat new approach to resistance training. The intent of this type of exercise is to improve and enhance your ability to function. For the businessperson this could translate to a better ability to climb stairs, get in and out of the car, or carry groceries into the house. For the athlete this can mean an enhanced ability to move on the court or field of play, as well as a significant reduction in the risk of injury.

Body control training is a great approach to training for virtually every healthy individual. It is also quite often used as a significant part of an injury rehabilitation regime. Body control exercises can be the entire focus of your training program, or a supplement to your regular workout routine.

Typically in a body control training program you should keep your resistance somewhat light and your repetitions high (10-16). This is especially true in the early stages of your training. As the title suggests, control is a key element to this type of program. Each of the body control exercises are performed in an unstable setting, and the key is for you to constantly seek to balance and control your body and movements. As you progress, your ability to execute each exercise will improve. Once you can perform a lift with relative ease you should then increase the resistance.

Day 1			
Exercise	**Sets**	**Repetitions**	**Rest Period**
Alt. Dumbbell Press	3	12-14	1 Min.
One Leg Row	3	12-14	1 Min.
Wobble Board Arnolds	3	12-14	1 Min.
Wobble Board Curls	3	12-14	1 Min.
Wobble Board Kickback	3	12-14	1 Min.
Airplane Lunge	4	12-14	1 Min.
Single Leg RDL	4	12-14	1 Min.

Day 2			
Exercise	**Sets**	**Repetitions**	**Rest Period**
Stability Ball Chest Press	3	12-14	1 Min.
Stability Ball Pullovers	3	12-14	1 Min.
Stability Ball Shoulder Flies	3	12-14	1 Min.
Stability Ball Curls	3	12-14	1 Min.
Stability Ball Kickback	3	12-14	1 Min.
Stability Ball Bulgarian Squats	4	12-14	1 Min.
Stability Ball Hamstring Curls	4	12-14	1 Min.

Day 3 (The Gauntlet – No rest between sets)		
Exercise	**Sets**	**Repetitions**
Pushup and Rotate	3	12-14
Lunge	3	12-14
Single Leg Row	3	12-14
Single Leg RDL	3	12-14
Curl into Arnold	3	12-14
Single Leg Triceps Ext.	3	12-14

IMPORTANT NOTE: One set of each exercise should be completed without any rest between exercises before progressing to the next set. A total of three rounds of the Gauntlet should be completed.

CHAPTER 13
Important Concluding Notes

Variety is a very important component of any worthwhile training routine. There are psychological, as well as physiological reasons to support this statement. Performing the same training regime day in and day out will create mental and physical boredom. If you do not vary your program your motivation to train may well suffer. Even if your motivation remains steadfast, your muscles will surely become bored. Your routine will no longer serve as a stimulus; thus adaptation will slow, or even stop. In other words, your body will see no reason to adapt, or become stronger. This is why a periodization approach and following the principle of progressive overload are so important.

There are numerous ways to incorporate variety into your routine. Cycles that are marked by different repetitions is perhaps the most common. It is also important, however, to include a mixture of exercises into your workout. Your goal should be to vary your training routine while maintaining a balance with consistency.

Also, keep in mind that a total training program should include cardiovascular work along with abdominal and core training. Athletes should focus on sport specific athletic development as well. For example, speed, quickness, body control and explosive movement training should be a constant part of the serious athlete's training regime.

Good luck with your training! Stay consistent, focused, and safe. Last, but not least, have fun on your journey to improved fitness.

Photo & Illustration Credits

Coverphotos: Ed Rosenberger (front- and backcover), Mark McKown (backcover)
Coverdesign: Birgit Engelen, Stolberg
Illustrations: Gary Briggs (p. 8), André Besgens
Photos: Ed Rosenberger, Danny Carr (p. 30, right), Mark McKown (p. 30, left)